Historical Association Studies

Occupied France
Collaboration and Resistance 1940–1944

WQE

00688664

Historical Association Studies

General Editors: Muriel Chamberlain and H.T. Dickinson

China in the Twentieth Century
Paul Bailey

The Agricultural Revolution
John Beckett

Class, Party and the Political System in Britain 1867–1914
John Belchem

The Ancien Régime
Peter Campbell

Decolonization: The Fall of the European Empires
M.E. Chamberlain

Gandhi
Anthony Copley

The Counter-Reformation
N.S. Davidson

British Radicalism and the French Revolution
H.T. Dickinson

From Luddism to the First Reform Bill: Reform in England 1810–1832
J.R. Dinwiddy

Radicalism in the English Revolution 1640–1660
F.D. Dow

British Politics Since 1945: The Rise and Fall of Consensus
David Dutton

The Spanish Civil War
Sheelagh M. Ellwood

Revolution and Counter-Revolution in France 1815–1852
William Fortescue

The New Monarchy: England, 1471–1534
Anthony Goodman

The French Reformation
Mark Greengrass

Politics in the Reign of Charles II
K.H.D. Haley

Occupied France: Collaboration and Resistance 1940–1944
H.R. Kedward

Secrecy in Britain
Clive Ponting

Women in an Industrializing Society: England 1750–1880
Jane Rendall

Appeasement
Keith Robbins

Franklin D. Roosevelt
Michael Simpson

Britain's Decline: Problems and Perspectives
Alan Sked

The Cold War 1945–1965
Joseph Smith

Bismarck
Bruce Waller

The Russian Revolution 1917–1921
Beryl Williams

The Historical Association, founded in 1906, brings together people who share an interest in, and love for, the past. It aims to further the study and teaching of history at all levels: teacher and student, amateur and professional. This is one of over 100 publications available at preferential rates to members. Membership also includes journals at generous discounts and gives access to courses, conferences, tours and regional and local activities. Full details are available from The Secretary, The Historical Association, 59a Kennington Park Road, London SE11 4JH, telephone: 071–735 3901.

Occupied France
Collaboration and Resistance 1940–1944

H. R. KEDWARD

BLACKWELL
Oxford UK & Cambridge USA

Copyright © H. R. Kedward 1985

First published 1985
Reprinted 1989, 1992

Blackwell Publishers
108 Cowley Road, Oxford, OX4 1JF, UK

Three Cambridge Center
Cambridge, Massachusetts 02142, USA

All rights reserved. Except for the quotation of short passages for the
purposes of criticism and review, no part of this publication may be
reproduced, stored in a retrieval system, or transmitted, in any form
or by any means, electronic, mechanical, photocopying, recording or
otherwise, without the prior permission of the publisher.

Except in the United States of America, this book is sold subject to the
condition that it shall not, by way of trade or otherwise, be lent, re-
sold, hired out, or otherwise circulated without the publisher's prior
consent in any form of binding or cover other than that in which it is
published and without a similar condition including this condition
being imposed on the subsequent purchaser.

British Library Cataloguing in Publication Data
A CIP catalogue record for this book is available from the British
Library.

Library of Congress Cataloging in Publication Data
Kedward, H. R. (Harry Roderick)
  Occupied France.

  Bibliography: p.
  Includes index.
  1. World War, 1939–1945—France. 2. World War, 1939–1945—
Underground movements—France. 3. World War, 1939–1945—
Collaborationists—France. 4. France—History—German occupation,
1940–1945. I. Title.
D802.F8K39   1985   940.53′44   84—28285
ISBN 0–631–13927–3 (pbk.)

Acc. No.

00688664

Class No. 944.
0816 KED

Typeset by Cambrian Typesetters, Frimley, Surrey
Printed in Great Britain by T.J. Press (Padstow) Ltd, Padstow, Cornwall.

Contents

1 Occupation

On 10 May 1940, Hitler turned his war machine against Western Europe, and three days later the tanks of General Heinz Guderian astonished the military world by breaching the Meuse where it wound through the heavily-wooded Ardennes. The French concrete fortifications known as the Maginot Line were bypassed, and the Germans drove a furrow of occupation across northern France, exposing the bulk of the French and British armies in Belgium to attack from the rear. There was nothing in the strategic thinking of the French or British to turn such a predicament into anything except a retreat, and at the end of May the massive withdrawal from Dunkirk began. The very fact that the evacuation was so heroic and remarkable was seen by many of the French as a wry comment on their ally's contribution to the war. Only in the act of retreating to their own shores, it was widely remarked, did the British show any sign of military talent. In return, British public opinion viewed the French failures, both military and civilian, first with dismay but increasingly with contempt. By the second week of June their verdict was that the French had been defeated not only by the Germans but by panic within their own ranks.

Relentlessly the symbols of French vitality and independence were broken. The government left Paris on 10 June for Bordeaux, passing the millions of old men, women and children already on the roads, whether in cars, pushing carts and wheelbarrows, or just trudging miserably through the heat and storms, with little or no food, and dwindling hope of reaching safety before being overtaken by the Germans. On 14 June the German army staged its Roman triumph in the capital through streets deserted by all Parisians, except the very few who came to marvel at the physical presence of the conquerors. Late on 16 June, the Prime Minister Reynaud handed power to the group led by the Commander-in-Chief, Weygand, and the eighty-four-year-old hero of the First World War, Marshal Pétain, and on 17 June Pétain announced to the nation that he had agreed to head a new government and was asking the Germans for

WQEIC LRC

an armistice. Meanwhile he called on the French to lay down their arms, and in religious phrases he offered his person as a gift to France to attenuate the country's deep misfortune. It was the beginning of a personal ascendancy which has no equal in recent French history, and when the Senators and Deputies met at the Casino in the spa town of Vichy on 10 July to vote overwhelmingly to give full powers to Pétain, their vote finalized a process which turned the military defeat of France into the Fall of the Third Republic. An unregulated authoritarian regime was substituted for the structures of parliamentary democracy.

For three days after the fall of Dunkirk, bells were rung throughout Germany. The order came directly from Hitler, who responded to the successive stages of the German victory in France with gestures of ecstatic delight and unconcealed enjoyment. His return to Berlin, after the French campaign was over, was glowingly recorded in a documentary film, which expressed in rapid sequences and shattering sound the full extent of Hitler's personal triumph. It was mounted as a festival, and even the sober act of dictating the terms of the armistice was staged as an epic celebration. With a theatrical display of historic revenge, many of the clauses of the Versailles Treaty, which had penalized Germany so harshly after the First World War, were now imposed on the French, including a reduction of the army to 100,000 men, and the French were brought to the same clearing in the forest of Compiègne where Foch and Weygand had presided over the surrender of Germany in 1918. It was here that the signing of the armistice took place on 22 June 1940, and three days later France was formally under German occupation.

The zone to be occupied by the German army was much larger than expected; it included the whole of the north and west of the country and extended down the Atlantic coast to the Spanish border. In the centre it reached a line just north of the Massif Central, and in the south small areas along the Italian border were given to the Italians to occupy, even though Mussolini's cynically timed declaration of war had brought him no military successes. The unoccupied zone of central and southern France was the least populated and poorest part of the country, with the exception of the prosperous town of Lyon and the industrial complex of Clermont-Ferrand, both of which the German troops had reached but now agreed to leave. The Mediterranean coast was also left untouched, enabling the French to preserve a doorway to their possessions overseas. In economic terms this southern zone was utterly dependent on the occupied zone for everything except wine and fruit, but it appeared from the armistice that French administration would still be intact even in the occupied areas, so that the imbalance of the two zones did not at first seem too problematic. People imagined that occupation would be a purely military phenomenon and they did not envisage it in either political or economic terms. It was also reassuring to the French that Hitler had laid no claim to the French navy nor to the French colonies and had not even mentioned Alsace-Lorraine. The armistice, even with the extensive occupation, could therefore be accepted in Pétain's words 'with honour', and although Hitler alone had decided the terms, there were public acts of thanksgiving to the Marshal for having saved France from what might have been a harsher settlement. The irony of this attitude seen in retrospect should not obscure its very real hold on the French public at the time, though the illusions were at their height for no more than two or three months.

During those months, from late June to September, the Germans skilfully exploited the popular resentment against the previous regime and the doubts about the British as unreliable or even perfidious allies. To citizens returning to the northern towns, from which the local authorities had often fled in advance of the population, the occupying German troops offered a degree of physical reassurance by establishing a basic food service, but also a personal reassurance that the war and the catastrophe had not been the fault of the ordinary French people but had been caused by 'Jewish politicians and financiers of the Third Republic', and by 'machinations from the City of London'. Propaganda through posters and leaflets encouraged families to trust their children to the German soldiers, who were quite explicitly not indulging in pillage and rape, and to resume as normal a life as possible pending an imminent treaty of peace which would be signed as soon as the British recognized the helplessness of their situation.

This assumption that Britain would soon capitulate was shared by German troops and French public alike until the events of 3 July, when the British navy shelled the French fleet in its North African harbour of Mers-el-Kébir and killed over 1,200 French sailors. The British had neither accepted in full the French reasons for demanding an armistice nor believed the French promises that the fleet would never be allowed to fall into German hands. To make sure that there was no debate on the issue they seized the French ships already in British ports and issued a set of alternatives to the commanders of the fleet in North Africa which proposed either that they sailed to British waters, or that they scuttled their ships, or that they faced destruction. The ultimatum, which was intended by Churchill and the British navy as a sign of forceful determination to pursue the war at all costs, was badly received by the French. Admiral Gensoul at Mers-el-Kébir rejected the terms, and the British under Admiral Somerville opened fire. The context was one of strained Anglo-French relations ever since the German invasion of Belgium and France or, even further back, of long-standing naval and colonial rivalry between the two nations, and the immediate result was a wave of anger and dismay which swept the whole of France and severely increased the receptivity of the French to the blandishments of the German occupiers. Underneath this anger there was also a realization that Mers-el-Kébir was a statement of British intent, so that Churchill's determination was registered at some level in the French consciousness, but, as French sailors from Mers-el-Kébir have said, the fleet might well have responded to a less arrogant approach, and Churchill could have increased his war potential without alienating the French population. This missed opportunity haunted the minds of the Anglophiles and those who were to work out an alternative strategy to defeatism and submission, while in Britain there was defiance but little satisfaction. The first expressions of anger in France were at best followed by mute incomprehension. In general the French turned further away from the war and concentrated single-mindedly on day-to-day survival and the search for some return to a semblance of acceptable normality.

At least ten million people are thought to have taken to the roads or the railways as the Germans pushed even deeper into northern and central France. This mass exodus (*exode*) resembled a migration of people unknown in Europe since the Dark Ages, and it was dominantly an experience of women, old people and children. Crammed into school buildings, encampments of all kinds, town halls and railway stations throughout the south and south-west, they waited miserably for permission to go home and pick up the pieces of their shattered lives. Newspapers filled pages with requests for information about lost children, and local bulletins were issued daily on the possibilities of applying for re-entry into the occupied zone. The division between the zones which had seemed a thin line on a map was gradually seen for what it really was, a military frontier which the Germans could close or open at will, and in the first weeks after the armistice it was opened only to selected workers and administrators whom the Germans decided were vital to the smooth recovery of basic industries and public services in Paris and the north. By leaving as many people as possible to French initiatives in the south, the Germans ensured that grievances about food and other provisions were directed against French rather than German authorities. It was part of their tactics for maximizing the effects of the war and defeat for which the French would be held responsible, and minimizing the effects of the occupation which could be held against themselves.

Those returning in July to their homes in the occupied zone found all tricolour flags removed from public buildings and replaced by Nazi insignia, street directions in bold German type, a curfew imposed from eight o'clock in the evening to six in the morning, total absence of French cars and lorries, and groups of Germans everywhere buying lavishly in the re-opening shops, riding from one tourist site to another, staging endless parades and holding concerts in the local bandstands. There seemed little evidence of a war mentality or preparations for invading Britain, and this apparent stability of the situation encouraged people to re-adapt as if to a permanently changed reality. The German officers in charge of occupying the different towns and villages initially took hostages as an insurance against acts of rebellion, but these were progressively released and the most overt acts of constraint in the first few weeks were those enforcing the curfew or, in Paris, those insisting that Parisians crossed the streets at regulated points.

As winter approached, the economic severity of the situation had increasing impact. The Germans set an exchange rate of 20 francs to the mark, eight francs higher than the market value before the defeat, and this enabled them to purchase most items at an absurdly low price. Shopkeepers had to accept the German currency and were obliged to serve Germans first, though not all German soldiers insisted on this. In industry the distribution of raw materials was dependent on German authorization since all communications and transport in the first months were rigorously controlled, and in mechanized agriculture the same problem of access to fuel and materials meant that the pace of recovery was largely in German hands. Labour was severely reduced, with one and a half million prisoners of war held by the Germans under the terms of the armistice, but jobs were scarce too at a time when so many industries and services were unable to restart their activities. Food was severely rationed and queues formed everywhere for everything. Substitute products and ingredients became the norm and stratagems for survival were avidly sought in ancient recipes and long-forgotten customs. Friends and relations in the countryside became very popular, window boxes were planted with vegetables, and space created on the balconies of flats for chickens, rabbits and even goats. Bicycles were at a premium, and as the months passed vehicles were adapted to alternative sources of energy, notably the use of reservoirs of gas and the conversion of wood and charcoal into the *gazogène*

5

burners which had been in existence on the fringe of the motor business since the 1920s.

The necessity of being inventive and persistent had an occasional levelling effect on French society, and certain characteristics of working-class lives were suddenly an advantage. People whose work had always started early in the morning were often at the front of queues, and those with close family ties to peasant producers were often more certain of an extra basket of food. The billeting of German officers also affected poorer people less, since the Germans looked first to the bigger houses. But money, influence and authority were still an overwhelming advantage in the struggle for survival, and class differences were exacerbated, particularly in Paris, by the contrast between the affluence in the restaurants where meat and butter could always be found at a price, and the poverty of those queueing endlessly for their rations. In winter the cold emphasized the differences still further, and if working people were seen buying the collaborationist press it was normally because the paper was good enough to roll up and use as slow-burning fuel in the single household stove. Despite the rationing of gas and the frequency of power cuts, those with money could depend on their central heating or could afford the coal and wood which was only available on the black market. It was said that bourgeois and working-class women could be seen side by side under the Paris trees in the deep snow of 1941–2 looking for dead twigs and branches – but the image was more sentimental than real.

What is of value in the image, however, is the reminder that it was women who not only carried the main burden of the *exode*, but once back home had to double their workload in the absence of the one and a half million men held prisoner. Again, as with class distinctions, it was less a question of *new* inequalities between men and women as of old ones perpetuated and extended. Because of the Vichy ideology towards women, which valued only women's family and reproductive lives, it was made difficult even in the occupied zone for mothers of young children to work, even when their husbands were prisoners of war, but the allowances for women in that position, although increased, were so inadequate that paid work of some kind was a necessity. Those who found employment had to work under a stigma, on top of the burdens of finding food and preparing meals; confronting the irony of an ideology which idealized women's position as homemakers.

Between work and home women also had to do most of the queueing, while the work that had always been allotted to them of cleaning, washing and cooking was made infinitely longer and

6

harder by the shortage or unavailability of basic materials. Many women from the towns have said that the absence of soap was the hardest aspect of daily life under the occupation; the dirt, grease and oil of the workplace remained impervious to the substitute materials which were sold for cleaning. Scrubbing the few clothes that her family possessed accounted for endless hours in a working woman's life, and figures prominently in the recollections of the period.

Class and gender differences were situated in the context of local differences which were accentuated perhaps more than any other by the occupation. The towns were the hub of the German presence. By comparison life in the countryside could seem relatively unaltered. But it was the relationship *between* the towns and the countryside which was substantially affected. The majority of the prisoners of war came from rural areas, and it was felt by peasant families that the workers in the towns had contributed little to the war. And yet they were thrown together by the dependence of the townspeople on extra food from the countryside, and this caused resentment to flow in the other direction. Stories of peasant greed circulated widely in the towns and it is difficult to evaluate the truth or falsity of such stories when the history of the period has been overwhelmingly written by town-dwellers. What is certain is that there was a regression in town–country attitudes to a more nineteenth-century relationship, something which is explained not just by the problems of food supply but also by the absence of transport and communication. When horse-drawn carriages and buses re-emerged in the Paris streets, people talked of a return to 1900; outside Paris the backward move seemed to go further. Kilometres were measured by the time it took to walk them and neighbouring villages became isolated from each other. Visits by town-dwellers were purely for food, and peasant producers no longer needed to go to the markets in the towns. With freedom of circulation limited to those with a German pass (*Ausweis*), anyone who came from the towns by car, or even by rail, was immediately suspect, and it does not seem an exaggeration to say that the life of the peasants returned for two or even three years to an ancient impenetrability.

Experience of the occupation was subject to these and many other variables. People in the two zones developed myths about each other. In the occupied zone it was imagined that everywhere in the south provisions were plentiful. In fact the towns situated in the mono-culture regions of the Mediterranean, where only wine or citrus fruits were produced, had far less to eat than those situated in areas of mixed farming in the north. Working people in Nice and Marseille came closer to desperate hunger than most other communities in urban France. In the centre of Paris the Jardins du Luxembourg were planted out with vegetables, but not all parts of Paris, nor many towns elsewhere, had either the space or the climate to make such adaptations.

It would be a mistake to imagine that the restrictions and the tightening of life under the occupation meant that a dull uniformity and grey repetition characterized most people's existence. Such a picture is an easy one to conjure out of the mass of references to the unrelieved problems of finding enough to eat, or fuel to burn or clothes to wear. But there were also irregularities and unpredictabilities which marked the occupation. Power cuts, the requisitioning of goods by a German commission, the sudden arrest of a co-worker, any of these might change the pattern of work for hours or even days. The curfew hours were frequently changed; transport available one day would be unavailable the next, and the German presence itself was liable to dramatic changes of mood. The least the French could do to mark their own presence was to 'narguer les Allemands', to irritate the Germans by minor gestures of defiance, made to look accidental or unthinking: knocking over a German's drink, misdirecting a German tourist, pretending not to hear or understand orders given in the street, or wearing combinations of clothes which made up the forbidden tricolour of blue, white and red. At any moment the reaction of the Germans might change from tolerance to repression, and in this sense the actions of everyday life had potential consequences far beyond their apparent insignificance.

The cinema was a place of just such unpredictability. Tightly controlled by the German army's Propaganda Abteilung, the cinemas were compelled to project German-made newsreels alongside the French films, and often a German documentary as well. The reaction of the French was not to boycott the cinemas, whose warmth and entertainment were vital to them, but to whistle, stamp or go outside during the newsreels. When German police were posted to control such activity they could not identify the ringleaders and demanded that the lights should be left on. This reduced any projected film to absurdity, so the lights were switched off again and the barracking of the films continued. But again, at any moment the Germans could arrest several rows of the audience at once, and in the later stages of the occupation cinemas were favoured by the Germans for arbitrary raids leading to mass arrests of men for compulsory labour service.

Not just in cinemas but everywhere, the French gradually realized they were facing not a strictly military presence with defined powers and limited intentions but an all-pervading authority which was steadily enlarging its capacity to influence, infiltrate and control. With every week that passed after the first two months of experimentation and mutual adjustment, the reality of being a defeated *and* occupied country forced the French to reappraise their initial reactions to the Germans. Where it had been common to acknowledge that the Germans were well-behaved, the phrase expressing the fact, 'les Allemands sont corrects', rapidly became a joke in poor taste, and a sullen resentment took its place. The armistice was first seen for the masquerade it was when it was realized that the Germans had annexed Alsace-Lorraine into the German Reich without any reference to the French government. The two provinces were intensively Germanized and submitted to every form of Nazi control, and the Alsace-Lorrainers thought to be hostile to assimilation, due to their loyalty to the French language and culture, were heaped into lorries and trains and driven into the unoccupied zone where they were dumped in their thousands without money or belongings. The brutal expulsions began as early as July 1940 and continued throughout the autumn, and Jews were differentiated from other French 'undesirables' only by the degree of harrassment and verbal insult to which they were subjected. In 1940 the Nazis were still favouring exile for Jews on the western edges of the Reich. Robert Wagner, the Gauleiter of Alsace, and Joseph Bürckel, the Gauleiter of Lorraine, both early recruits to the Nazi party, carried out the Germanization, and Aryanization, with a mixture of force, cajolery and material incentives, but neither succeeded in reconciling their province to German rule, and the reasons for their failure were merely a variant on the failure of German authorities elsewhere in France. They talked of integrating France into a New Europe and a New Order, they appealed for cooperation and volunteers, but as the war intensified and expanded rather than ending as they had confidently predicted, they could not conceal the view of Hitler, Goering, Himmler and Goebbels that France was a country to be exploited and controlled and that the Nazi leaders had no concept of what a New Europe might be beyond a vast pool of labour and resources for the Thousand Year Reich.

It had already been apparent to opponents of Nazism in the 1930s that Hitler was more than just another German autocrat. What historians now call the primacy of politics and ideology in the Nazi regime was widely observed in the six or seven years leading up to Hitler's war. But in 1940 the image of Hitler as an avenging German nationalist, turning the tables on the Versailles powers and re-establishing Germany as the centre of Europe, was the dominant one in France, eclipsing the image of Nazism as a new and fanatical ideology. In the first few months of occupation all the stereotypes of German culture and behaviour were to be seen. Prussian bearing, the musical German, the thoroughness of German administration, the German respect for culture and the physical attributes of the blond and muscular men and women, all were clearly recognized and discussed by the French as they took stock of the occupiers. French soldiers who had occupied parts of Germany after 1918 made comparisons with their own occupation in an almost neutral manner and allusions to the see-saw pattern of military victory from 1870 to 1940 were commonplace. According to de Gaulle, Pétain himself, in the period shortly before his access to power, acknowledged that it was Germany's turn to win.

But the French know the main points of their national history well, and it was increasingly observed that Bismarck and Moltke's occupation following the Franco-Prussian war had been substantially different.

Paul Simon, in an account of Paris and the occupation written in early 1942, wrote:

> In 1871 the Germans occupied only; this time they are interfering in everything. They have installed themselves in the railways, public administration, police forces, banks, insurance companies, press, wireless, films, law and education. They are everywhere, even in the so-called unoccupied zone, and in the colonies under the guise of the Armistice Commissions.
>
> They are not only imposing a form of government on the French, but also choosing men for that government; nominating civil servants, making laws, imposing fines, raising money, suppressing all liberty, even of thought, and forcing France into one-sided collaboration.
>
> A regime of tyranny has been set up . . . The prisons are full, and every day fresh executions take place.
>
> This is Hitler's 'New Order' for bringing happiness to other nations. (Simon, 1942, p. 27)

With all that we now know about Nazism this seems all too obvious and even understated. Yet in France between 1940 and 1942 this had to be discovered and realized, often reluctantly and painfully, by those who felt the situation was uncomfortable but tolerable in 1940 and thought that the Germans were only asserting their historic rights as occupiers of a conquered nation. Slowly the political and ideological dimensions of the occupation became the major reality, putting the day-to-day problems of food, fuel and money into a different perspective. The understanding that the French people had

10

of the occupation went through three stages. First, it was the consequence of French defeat and French failures; second, it was the heavy presence of Germans with all their national characteristics; and third, it was an ideological domination by a tyrannical Nazism. Not all French people moved through these three stages: some stayed in stage one or stage two and some started in stage three. Nor were the stages coextensive with dates or clearly defined periods. In some parts of occupied France the presence of a traditional army commander with musical interests and a code of military honour gave the local population a period of protection from Nazi ideology.

The first clandestine novel to be published by the Resistance, *Le Silence de la Mer* by Vercors (1942), accepted that such honourable, cultured Germans were present in France, but alerted the French to the dangers of believing that such a musical German was typical of the occupiers. Behind him were the Nazi fanatics, enemies not just of France but of the humanism within the German tradition of Goethe and Beethoven. The novel initially disturbed several resisters by the sympathetic portrait of the musical officer in question, Werner von Ebrennac, but it was just this sympathy which made the officer's discovery of the true nature of his own leaders such a powerful end to the novel. Taking a German rather than a French person through the realization that it was a Nazi occupation and not a benevolent German one was more than a literary device. It brilliantly served the necessities of Resistance propaganda, but it also registered a reality which historians have since endorsed in full. There were major divisions of attitudes and intentions within the German occupation, but the Nazi politics and ideology, though not in obvious control from the start, were soon in a position of dominant power even if their influence was unevenly exerted throughout France. The Vercors story is as much a document as a novel.

While military commanders were controlling the return of populations, and assuring an orderly start to the occupation, a young lieutenant, Helmut Knochen, was establishing the presence of the SS and Gestapo in Paris. Army leaders had complained to Hitler that the SS and the Secret Police had caused difficulties in the military campaign against Poland, and out of residual respect for traditional army opinion Hitler did not force the political issue when it came to the invasion of France. Himmler accepted a subsidiary role but made sure that Knochen entered Paris in the baggage of the German army, and that a labyrinth of agents and informers was secretly created. A more senior SS officer, Dr Thomas, was added to the staff after a few weeks, but when his provocative tactics towards the French population upset the military command he was withdrawn. It was hardly a defeat for the SS for by then the Gestapo was too solidly entrenched to be checked. The hysterical racist, Theodor Dannecker, had arrived in September 1940 as the direct representative of Adolf Eichmann, and while Knochen infiltrated Parisian society Dannecker made contacts with the French anti-semites and fascists. Between them they filed a mass of details on the existence of German refugees, Jews, communists, freemasons and 'enemies of the Reich', and set up intricate cross-channels of power and communication with the Abwehr and the Geheime Feldpolizei, the authorized military organization in charge of counter-espionage and military security. Both the Abwehr and the Gestapo set up commercial concerns to camouflage their operations, which is how they penetrated into the unoccupied zone, but in 1941 they came increasingly into the open as the opposition of the French people moved into a new phase following Hitler's invasion of Russia. The Gestapo was more equipped to meet this new phase than the military police since it already had archives bulging with details about the French communists. As a result, power swung decisively behind the political police, and in May 1942 Himmler appointed General Karl Oberg to be 'head of the SS and the Police' in France, and installed him with full military ceremony.

The German army of occupation administered by General Otto von Stülpnagel was not the only loser to the growing power of the SS and Gestapo. The political wing of the occupation under the German Ambassador Otto Abetz also saw a relative diminution of power, but in this case there was less disagreement than rivalry. Abetz was unusual in the Nazi hierarchy in having a French wife, in being something of an internationalist and pacifist, and in being politically left of centre. He had made close French friends before the war in the Comité France-Allemagne which continued to favour Franco-German exchanges and cooperation after Hitler had come to power. He therefore had a ready-made circle of French contacts, and developed these into the nearest approximation to a pioneer group for the New Europe that the occupation produced. This did not make him a model for von Ebrennac in the Vercors novel. On the contrary, his pursuit of an understanding between France and Germany was subordinate to the imposition of Nazi ideals on French society. He organized the censorship of all media, and was in charge of all political relations with the government of Marshal Pétain, as the Vichy regime was most commonly known in the first few months. He was answerable directly to Ribbentrop and Hitler, and his usefulness to them was due to his energy and enthusiasm in trying to persuade the French of the value and superiority of Nazi ideas. He was the diplomatic face of the New Order prepared to argue that Hitler was interested in the cooperation of France even when he knew that the opposite was essentially the case.

For French ministers and administrators, particularly the Prefects, there was an obvious difference between the purely military commanders, the political representatives of Abetz, and the dangerously threatening agents of the SS and the Gestapo. Archives of Vichy personnel and departments show the complexity of their relationships, which were cordial with some of the occupiers and suspicious or hostile with others. The German archives show the same diversity from their side. But from the point of view of most French people the occupation came to be seen as a single phenomenon, with a unity of purpose and design, albeit with a multiplicity of agents. Officially it was the Gestapo who launched the arrests of Jews and carried out the mass deportations which began in 1942, whereas officially it was the army command who arrested anyone accused of sabotage or active opposition to the occupying authorities, but the distinction meant little to the Jewish victims, to the resisters or to the innocent hostages shot by the military in reprisal for any French attack on their own personnel. The composite brutality of the German occupation remains a more lasting image than any indeterminate notions of separate spheres of authority.

A question which always arises when discussing the occupation is whether the increasingly unpleasant realities of the Nazi presence made a significant difference to the day-to-day preoccupations of the French. It is not difficult to discern a certain level of contempt in many memoirs and histories of the period for the way in which, under the occupation, cafés continued to function, plays were staged, films were made and projected, popular songs were sung, sport was enjoyed as never before, and routine domestic life centred on the permanent struggle with the Ministry of Provisions. In the same vein it is often pointed out that night clubs were quickly back in business after the defeat, that horse racing started again at Auteuil on 12 October 1940, that romantic love was seen to flourish, that illegitimate births increased, and that film stars commanded more publicity than in the golden years of Hollywood's silent screen. Such a list of observations could be extended indefinitely by moving out of the towns, and particularly out of Paris, to indicate the continuity of gossip in the village square and the continuing presence of what the urban administrators called 'the incurable egoism of the peasant'.

It is not the accuracy of such observations which provokes discussion and disagreement, but the fact that the same details of everyday life can be used to suggest *either* an almost treasonable indifference to the occupation *or*, on the contrary, a heroic determination to maintain French life and vitality in the face of the occupiers. In some ways the argument is merely part of a wider disagreement about the value that should be attached to everyday life at any period of history. There are always some historians who are ready to give the everyday lives of people a positive quality and see them as full of character and value, while others treat them as insignificant or even contemptible. But the problem of daily life under the occupation goes a little further. In Britain, where there was no occupation but where the brutality of the Nazi war machine made a severe impact in the bombing of civilians, there is little debate in assessing the day-to-day activities of the population. When the milk bottles were distributed as usual to the bombed houses of Coventry, or when the theatres of London insisted that the show must go on, no one accused the British people of a ritual obsession with fresh milk or an indifference of theatre-goers to the carnage outside. There is a consensus on the meaning of such acts. In France, on the other hand, the severe divisions caused by the defeat and occupation ensured that no such consensus emerged either at the time or since. The customary disagreements over the value of *la vie quotidienne* were perpetuated and intensified.

For this reason there can be no simple conclusion about the French day-to-day existence under the occupation, and no single answer to the question of whether or not the severity of the Nazi presence was directly reflected in daily behaviour. This is not always admitted in the histories of the period, but it is well expressed in much of the imaginative work on the occupation in novels, plays and films. Roger Vailland's novel *Drôle de jeu* (1945) and François Truffaut's film *Le Dernier Métro* (1980) both acknowledge the difficulty in ascribing clear-cut values to routine behaviour, and Henri Amouroux's studies of French life under the occupation come close to fictional treatments, not because he invents anything, but because he is highly sensitive to the importance and ambiguity of daily activities.

The stress and uncertainty of the occupation for most French people were such that there was a natural tendency to look towards things that were familiar and reassuring. The preparation, consumption and discussion of food had always been, and still is, a marked feature of ordinary French life, and it is anything but surprising to see that feature given even more emphasis during the occupation. This does not invalidate such satires as *Au bon beurre* (1952), Jean Dutourd's scathingly funny account of a dairy shop in occupied Paris, since there were undoubtedly some people who thought of nothing else but lining their stomachs and filling their shelves, but it does discredit the view that the pursuit of food was, by itself, a sign of indifference to the wider issues of the occupation. The same can be said of any other daily activity, providing it did not involve the exploitation of other people's hardship, or feed parasitically on the difficulties of the time.

Those who did exploit the needs of others and became the parasites of the occupation were often the first to be recruited as agents and informers by the German police. Though ostensibly opposed to the black market and to racketeering in industry, the Germans became increasingly dependent on the services which racketeers could provide as the attitude of the French population hardened against them. It was this German connection which finally destroyed many black marketeers, rather than the moral outrage of people at having to pay exorbitant prices. Due to the organizational failures or incapacities of the French Ministry of Provisions, less than half of the available food in the country was distributed through officially approved channels. The black market was a vast unco-ordinated area of business in which the remainder was bought and sold. Most people at some time had recourse to the black market to supplement their rations, and it was even argued that if more provisions were brought into the official markets, the Germans would find it easier to requisition larger amounts of food and resources. They exacted the astronomical sum of 400 million francs a day from the French authorities, which met the costs of the occupation ten times over, and in addition requisitioned whatever they needed for the war economy. Most French people in the production business, whether agricultural or industrial, were pre-pared to hide their stocks, camouflage their products or distort their figures of production in order to minimize their liability to German requisitions, and the same process kept them from declaring the full extent of their output to French inspectors. It was a knife-edge strategy, for the result could be a reduction in resources and manpower, enforced by various industrial and agricultural commis-sions, but with such a pervasive need to produce, and yet not to sell in the open market, it was understandable that the black market became structural to the occupied French economy. It was an operation in which the traders differed more in degree than in substance, and at the Liberation the French public recognized this fact. Where the major profiteers and those who had closely served the Germans were denounced, if not always caught, there remained a mass of smaller people whose smaller profits were more or less assimilated into the necessities of war.

By 1942 the occupation had become an intricate system of political and ideological control, and to endure it the French had developed equally intricate mechanisms of survival. They had also developed the utterly opposed reactions of collaboration and resistance, and the events of 1942 enabled most French people for the first time to appreciate the choice which lay before them. In March of that year the German Government, through its special Minister of Labour, Fritz Sauckel, extended the pressure of the occupation by demanding the recruitment of French workers for factories in Germany; in August and September the racial policy of the Final Solution was extended to France, and the first barbaric scenes of mass deportation of Jews gave a terrible twist to the meaning of Hitler's war; and in November the occupation itself was extended to the whole of the country. Neither at this point, nor at any other, was any concern shown by the Germans for the terms of the armistice, and the French could legitimately claim that despite the armistice the Germans were still waging war against the French people. But this was not a claim made by the regime at Vichy.

2 Vichy

The relief which French people experienced when Pétain called for a ceasefire was widespread if not universal. But it was mixed with many other feelings. Neville Lytton, an English artist, was living in France at the time and he described the reaction in a small republican community not far from the Swiss frontier:

> Most of us were old war comrades and we could hardly believe our ears when we heard the aged Marshal's trembling voice telling us that he was making an appeal for an armistice – an armistice with honour as between soldiers. How could Pétain mention the word 'honour' and the word 'Hitler' in the same sentence, and how could he, an old soldier, mistake this satanic creature for a soldier? ... Well might Hitler, this ersatz Caesar, exclaim 'Veni, Vidi, Vichy'.
>
> When his speech was over I looked round and tears were rolling down the rugged cheeks of these war veterans, many of them bearing traces of grievous wounds. (Lytton, 1942, p. 17)

Tears of shame and humiliation, also of anger. Lytton's account was written in 1942, and since then most recollections have mentioned the tears, but tears also of gratitude, pride in Pétain's courage and pity for the old soldier in his act of self-sacrifice. Everyone remembers that broadcast, and they remember exactly where they were at the time. What they often forget is that it was not made from Vichy, but from Bordeaux. No one had yet thought of Vichy as a place of government. First there was Pétain, then there was Vichy. This was the order of events, and this remained the order of people's allegiance, or at least the allegiance of those who did not reject them both. It was also the order that the Vichy ministers, administrators and publicists promoted. Pétain was 'the great leader' and 'the father': he was to be adulated, and followed with blind obedience. According to Charles Maurras, leader of the nationalist movement Action Française, the decisions of Pétain could not even be discussed. His word was beyond dispute (Maurras, 1941, p. 287).

The military career of Philippe Pétain before the First World War had been undistinguished, and in the climate of aggressive war fever in 1914 he was something of an outsider. Cautious about any quick resolution of the war, he argued that defence would be the operative word, and indeed as the war settled into a stalemate in the trenches he received recognition of his views and was rapidly promoted as someone who embodied the necessary virtues of patience and endurance. He was also more humanitarian than many of the other war leaders and in 1916–17, the crucial years of maximum revolt against the war, he tempered punishment with concessions in his suppression of army mutinies. He advised better food, longer periods of leave and quicker promotion for those at the front, and this understanding of the mentality of the ordinary soldier was as important as his defence of Verdun in giving him an unassailable reputation for leadership among the 'anciens combattants'. For his own part he emerged from the war believing himself to have been proved correct in every aspect of his thinking – an illusion of infallibility which eventually grew into a self-esteem little short of narcissism, enabling him to promote himself as the embodiment of France and receive the most extravagant tributes as his due.

Generalizing from his war successes, Pétain claimed a particular relationship with truth, and in the inter-war years became convinced that the loose hold of the Third Republic on the loyalty of the people was due to the incapacity of politicians to tell what was true from what was false. As a result, he believed the public had not been honestly led into war in 1939, but dishonestly misled into defeat, and his first statements as head of government at the end of June 1940 promised the people that he would always tell them the truth. Abstract values and absolutes flourish at a time of crisis and the Marshal's promises were received by the majority of the French people without any of the scepticism with which they would have greeted such statements from a political leader before the war. In fact they did not see him as a political personality at all but as someone above politics, despite his debt to the nationalist doctrines of Action Française, despite his post as Minister of Defence in the highly conservative government of Gaston Doumergue in 1934, and despite his most recent appointment as ambassador to Spain after the Civil War when he demonstrated a close sympathy with Franco's regime. Such was the disarray of France in June 1940 that these political affinities counted as an unbiased perspective on national events and Pétain was widely seen as a leader for all the French and not just for those on the Right.

This was no less than the creation of a myth. Pétain was

mythologized in a way which corresponds closely to the analysis of myths made later by Roland Barthes (1957). In the first place the myth was essentially anti-historical. Pétain's leadership qualities had developed over time in such a way that they were specific qualities linked to his sense of military value and right-wing concepts of nationalism. This specific, historical development was rarely, if ever, mentioned, and the press was even told not to refer to him continually as the victor of Verdun, for this accentuated his age and pointed to an event which was no longer 'relevant'. Instead his qualities were projected as natural and universal and not as specific.

Secondly, Pétainism was identified with common sense and realism. No argument against Pétain could start from a sound basis: it was made to look absurd, and people who objected to his leadership were 'flying in the face of fact'. It was taken for granted that he had made all the right, sensible decisions. To deny this was to go beyond the bounds of reason and good sense. Thirdly, it immobilized choice. At any given moment Pétain was credited with having looked carefully at all the alternatives. There was therefore no point in looking for oneself at these alternatives or imagining there was a different choice that could be made. This aspect of the myth allowed people to say that if something was worth doing the Marshal would have done it, and if he had not done it then, by definition, it could not have been worth doing.

This cult of the Marshal was the nearest France came to unity in defeat. It cut across political divisions, it linked generations, and it appeared to bring town and country together. His tours round the unoccupied zone brought huge crowds into the city squares and lined the country roads with peasant admirers. He was welcomed in person by hundreds of thousands, and millions more displayed his portrait in their homes. It showed a handsome, kindly, military face with sriking blue eyes which belied his eighty-four years, and it became an icon in the family religion of a France which had fallen back on Bonapartist values of the charismatic hero 'l'homme providentiel.'

Destructuring the myth, breaking out of the irrational hold that Pétainism had established over people's loyalties, involved reasserting the historical perspective, seeing Pétain as a political leader of a particular kind, challenging the assumptions about common sense, and making a personal choice after weighing all the possibilities. In the summer of 1940 very few people set out to undermine the position of Pétain in this way, and the lack of articulated opposition enabled him to use his undisputed leadership to initiate a political programme designed to transform French society at all levels. He called it a

National Renovation but it was more usually known as the National Revolution, and the ministers he picked for his government at Vichy were entrusted with this radical task of revolutionizing France from above. To many of them it seemed less of a political task than a historic mission.

The discreet and somnolent spa town of Vichy was an unlikely setting for an energetic crusade. It was chosen mainly for its surfeit of hotels in which the ministries could spread themselves after their cramped quarters en route from Bordeaux. Once Pétain and his government had decided to settle there, people from the world of business, journalists, acolytes, and fixers of all kinds transformed the nature of the town. For several months at least Vichy was indeed the centre of France. Everyone was there, and even after the senators and deputies had cast the votes which abolished the Third Republic and inaugurated the Vichy regime many kept a foothold in the town to see what the transitional stages would bring. Pétain himself preferred the Hôtel du Parc to the elegant little château of Madame de Sévigné, and in the hot days of July and August the crowds assembled at regular hours every day to see the Marshal take his walk from the hotel into the park, where he would greet old soldiers and lift small children up to his chest. In the same hotel were the Foreign Ministry and the Ministry of Information, and for the Council of Ministers the crowd was rewarded by the incongruous sight of Pétain side by side with Pierre Laval, the maverick politician of the Third Republic who was quickly known in Vichy for disagreeing with Pétain on almost every subject.

Why was Pierre Laval appointed to Pétain's government? At the beginning of the First World War, the careers of the two men could hardly have been more polarized: Pétain the cautious, defensive military leader, Laval, over twenty-five years younger, a barrister and youngest socialist deputy. After the war Laval broke with the Socialist party and became a one-man party of his own, calling himself an independent socialist. As such he became mayor of Aubervilliers, a working-class suburb of Paris, was elected to the Senate and held various ministerial posts, including the premiership from June 1935 to January 1936. During the 1930s he pursued his constant theme of peaceful coexistence in Europe through negotiation with anyone and everyone including Mussolini, the British and Stalin. He was a tough and successful negotiator, but he saw his efforts frustrated by shifts of policy as governments changed, and by 1940, having opposed every policy which led to the declaration of war, he was angrily contemptuous of parliamentary democracy. Laval described the war as an unmitigated disaster and when the defeat confirmed his view, he quickly drew the political lessons and made sure that his voice was forcefully heard at Bordeaux. He argued for a negotiated peace and for a total change of regime which would eliminate the parliamentary system. From contrasting careers and attitudes in 1914 he and Pétain had reached remarkably similar positions in June 1940. Although they were still polar opposites in many aspects of their personalities, they stood side by side, or face to face, as two independently minded, self-confident men, both believing they had been proved right by history, both sure that they were the right person for the crisis, Pétain as spiritual leader and Laval as a redoutable negotiator, and both committed to a settlement of the disastrous war and a transformation of the parliamentary regime into an autocracy. Who used who in this situation is impossible to determine. They both used each other; Pétain used the tactical skills of Laval to convince uncertain politicians that he should be given full powers, and Laval used the enormous prestige of Pétain to allay the democrats' fears of a personal autocracy. The vote of 10 July was a triumph for them both, but the mistake should not be made of seeing one as more politically-minded than the other. They adopted different political roles, complementary to each other.

Together they initiated the expansive programme of internal reconstruction, in which Pétain was most interested, and the programme of coexistence with Germany which is where Laval took the lead. They were both involved in each other's operations. Laval showed scepticism towards the more reactionary ideals of the National Revolution but signed any necessary decrees which put them into practice, and Pétain showed caution towards Laval's negotiations with Abetz in Paris, but was himself interested in a meeting with Hitler well before he agreed to go with Laval to meet Hitler at Montoire on 24 October 1940. It was their personal incompatibility which finally forced the issue at the end of the year. By then other ministers were scheming to get rid of Laval, and Pétain fell in with the plot and dismissed him on 13 December. Public opinion, which had been alarmed by the implications of the meeting of Pétain and Hitler, welcomed the dismissal of Laval as a reassertion of Pétainist independence and nationalism over the machinations of Laval, but within a few months Admiral Darlan, Laval's eventual replacement, was offering more to the Germans than Laval had done, and throughout 1941 Pétain increasingly accepted the arguments which Laval had advanced that France should negotiate a strong position for herself in Nazi-occupied Europe.

Eventually in April 1942 Laval was returned to power, with Pétain still ambivalent towards him, and what that return meant, together with the history of Vichy's relations with Germany, will be looked at in the next chapter. The history of those relations is the one on which Vichy is ultimately judged, but the priority in the minds of most Vichy ministers and Pétain himself was the creation not of a new Europe but a new France. This task dominated the activity of the Vichy administrators during the first two years from 1940 to 1942, years in which the Vichy government had a quite unprecedented freedom in the area of internal policy, unchecked as it was by any parliamentary system. Laval told Pétain that he had more power than Louis XIV, and Pétain liked to quote that fact in ministerial meetings.

In theory, Vichy's administration also extended across the occupied zone, but it was subject to German interference and veto, so that the south was the only area fully controlled by the Marshal's government. Here Vichy's scenario for a national renaissance was staged with an intensive series of decrees and laws which installed a bedrock of Pétainist disciples at all levels of the administration, idealized the family and peasant life, mobilized youth into the service of nationalism, and dissolved, repressed and victimized the elements of society which were thought to have caused the decadence of France. It was an assertive mixture of heady idealism about the immediate future and sweeping revenge on the recent past.

The intellectual origins of this ambitious programme lay in thinkers and writers who had articulated a spiritual challenge to Revolutionary France. Against the values of Liberty, Equality and Fraternity they preached an organic society in which people respected their place, in which discipline at work and the preservation of rural life dictated the rhythm of change, and from which flowed stability, a flourishing family life and the greatness of the nation. The Catholic Church was revered as a model for moral leadership, community life and obedience, and political health was equated with strong authoritarian government, never with the fratricidal struggle of groups, factions and parties. The old regions of France were preferred to the new *départements* as representing in a more authentic way the grass-roots culture and traditions of the people, and class struggle was rejected as yet one more abstract and artificial concept invented to divide the nation. Whether from de Maistre, Bonald, Frederic Le Play, La Tour du Pin, Maurice Barrès, Charles Maurras, General Lyautey or Albert de Mun, their ideas were cohesive enough to have formed a permanent alternative to Republican thought, an *alter ego* of French society in the seventy years preceding the advent of Vichy.

22

But political ideas do not come only from intellectuals: they are also the expression of social position and economic interest, and the National Revolution with its populist slogan – Travail, Famille, Patrie – was firmly grounded in the values held by many within the upper and middle classes. At no point was it a purely intellectual exercise. Nor did it relate solely to a distant, pre-revolutionary past. It drew confidence, if not substance, from the success of the authoritarian, nationalist movements in Italy, Portugal, Spain and, most recently, Germany, and built on the backlash within France to the left-wing successes of the Popular Front. This backlash had strengthened in the two years before 1940, and at local level had projected people of social substance and influence into active political involvement, many of them for the first time.

Rapidly after 15 July 1940 these local 'notables' were put into the town halls and onto local councils to replace the political Left. They set about improving the assistance, shelter and organization vital to the refugees, and began the extensive operation of sending parcels to the prisoners of war and caring for their destitute families. It was initially an apolitical activity in which people from all parties were involved before the vote of 10 July. After that date it became identified as the first battle in the Pétainist crusade, and the credit that went to the notables for their considerable humanitarian efforts was credit for the Vichy government and Pétain. These new leaders of the communes and towns of France were from small industry and finance, from local businesses, and landed property and from high-status professions and most had an explicit interest in reversing, or at least stemming, the social changes of 1936. They became known in the prefects' reports to the Ministry of the Interior as 'the healthy elements of the population', but they were far from being a mandarin group or a small political minority. Just under 50 per cent of the all-male electorate had voted against the Popular Front in 1936, the last elections to be held before the war, and the Vichy propagandists could well speculate in the summer of 1940 that, had there been an election after the defeat, the result would have been a landslide to the Right. Pétainism in a sense, *was* that landslide, and just as there was little protest against Pétainism so at first there was no open rebellion against the arrival of a socially conservative or even reactionary class to all positions of power. For the first time since the Second Empire of Napoleon III, France had a uniformity of political control not just at national but at local level. From a nationalist perspective this was an essential reform if a strong executive were to enforce itself in all corners of the nation, but it meant that towns which had an ingrained left-wing consciousness were now administered entirely

23

from above against the political preferences of the locality. This made a nonsense of the Marshal's promise that he would restore the nation to the people who lived and worked at the grass roots. In many areas of the south, particularly in Languedoc, where there was a strong left-wing tradition in small towns and in the countryside, the result was to take government even further away from the people, and to open a credibility gap which was wider than anything produced by the Third Republic. It also meant that once the shock of the defeat had lost its paralysing force, any revival in left-wing attitudes had to be expressed in unauthorized and clandestine political operations, and in that way Vichy's political uniformity, like that of the Second Empire, encouraged opponents to become subversive, since all overt and peaceful ways of expressing political differences were blocked.

Uniformity in the town halls and prefectures ironically weakened one of the central policies in Vichy's own Revolution. Although many of the 'notables' had property in the countryside, whether farms, vineyards or just estates, they were not adequate representatives of the peasantry. Who, in fact, in modern French history had ever adequately represented the peasantry? And yet Vichy propaganda and Pétain himself promoted the peasant as the model for a revitalized France. Peasants were seen to possess 'heroic patience', 'a natural spiritual equilibrium', 'the essence of economic endeavour', 'the wisdom of the ages' (all phrases from Pétain's broadcasts). These speeches would not have been heard in the humble peasant cottages idealized by the Vichy regime, because very few peasants could afford a radio. But gathered round a set in a small village café they heard themselves extolled, and not surprisingly came to expect preferential treatment from the regime. It came in theory, but rarely in practice, for policy had to be mediated through an administrative hierarchy which was no less urban-based than under the Third Republic, and by 1942 the local notables of Vichy were referring to peasants as egoistic and obstructive.

Prefects were told to reanimate regional customs and peasant folklore, but while these prefects patronized village festivals and led the rustic dancing which followed the harvest, the peasants were demanding mechanization, spare parts for machinery, liquid fertilizer, and artificial insemination for their animals. Throughout the 1930s the French peasantry had struggled against their own diversity and isolation to create a political presence in the Republic. It was the start of an agricultural assertiveness which tolerated Vichy romanticism no more willingly than any other misconstruction of their needs. Peasants were flattered by Vichy's attention, and inspired by

Pétain; they were appeased by small subsidies and minor tax concessions; and they were glad to be protected in 1942–3 from conscription to labour service in Germany. But Vichy was ultimately judged by economic results, and the Ministry of Agriculture could do nothing to offset the crucial insufficiency of materials, seeds, animal foods and fertilizers caused by the German occupation and requisitions. It is estimated that 13 percent of the active peasantry was killed or taken prisoner in 1940, and although youth organizations and unmarried women were drafted into agricultural labour, there was a permanent shortage of skills. Production, for all these reasons, fell dramatically, and much of the real relationship between Vichy and its peasantry lay in the increasingly embittered process of getting the countryside to meet the basic needs of the towns. Once the compulsory labour service in Germany was extended to certain categories of rural workers, the relationship broke down altogether. By 1942 Vichy's rural policy of a return to the land (*retour à la terre*) was already threadbare. By 1943–4 it was in tatters.

The idealized peasant wife, the woman both on the land and in the home, feeding the chickens and nurturing her large family, was an image which stood for Vichy's policy both towards the countryside and towards the family. Breeding became a sacred duty, a national obligation, and women were seen as mothers first, above all else. It was not a new perspective on women, nor was the demographic obsession of Vichy a sudden eruption of consciousness and concern. The French birth rate had fallen far behind that of other industrializing countries of Europe, and in 1914 it was realized that the ratio of Germans to French was three to two. In fact in military terms it was worse, and the ratio of young Germans aged twenty to their equivalent in France was 22 to 10. By 1940, attempts by the Third Republic to stimulate family growth, culminating in major concessions to mothers *and* fathers of large families, had failed to alter the imbalance, and Vichy believed that an authoritarian campaign could succeed where the Republic had failed. Its sympathizers claim it was proved right, since in 1943 births showed an upward trend, and Vichy believed this was entirely due to the new moral climate. Sceptics have suggested that the long evenings at home due to the curfew were the major cause, but women themselves have said two things. In the first place they have pointed out that Vichy improved pre-natal provisions and post-natal care, and women were now given credit for a function which had always been taken for granted by patriarchal society. Secondly they have said that in the darkest days of the occupation a baby was a sign of hope.

Credit was also given to women for staying at home, with or

without a family, and early in the autumn of 1940 measures were enacted to prevent married women from going out to work. On 7 July, a few days before the existence of the Vichy regime, the government of Pétain told prefects to encourage local businesses to sack their women workers who were married to demobilized soldiers, and this was done even where the husband was unemployed and the family was dependent on the wife's wages. This began a pattern of increased discrimination in the workplace against all women, and their wages for equal work were pegged further than ever behind that of men, while in education examiners were told to pass fewer girls than boys at the *baccalauréat*.

Eventually the idealized Vichy woman suffered much the same fate as the idealized peasant. Her subsidies for staying at home and having children appeared initially to give her a new stature. However traditional it was, however subjugated to male dominance, it seemed preferable to be rewarded for staying at home than to be expected to do it as a matter of course, without rewards, subsidy or any public commendation. But by the winter of 1941–2, which was the worst since the 1890s, the subsidies were quite inadequate to compensate for the hardships and the loss of outside work, and in 1943–4 Laval made a significant departure from Vichy policy and began to look to compulsory female labour to replace the men who had been sent to Germany. It was a final sign that women were essentially to be manipulated, and in this sense Vichy showed continuity with previous regimes rather than change. It was the elevated moral tone and the spiritual justification that were different.

Vichy policies towards the land and the family encompassed both the unoccupied and the occupied zone, but this was not the case for the youth camps, nor for the association of ex-soldiers, the Légion des Anciens Combattants. Neither of these crucial aspects of the National Revolution was approved by the German authorities, and the extension of them into the north was forbidden. The Légion was an amalgamation of the fragmented associations of ex-soldiers which had existed before the war, and was launched to link Pétain with the people to whom he felt most immediate affinity. It quickly became a popular vanguard for the ideals of the National Revolution, organizing the receptions for Pétain on his tours across the southern zone and creating welfare links with prisoners of war and their families. Although it watched the local press for any signs of weakening in the Pétainist resolve, it never became the single political party equivalent to those in the fascist regimes, but it was seen by many as a close approximation.

Members of the Légion had privileged access to jobs and

promotion, and in some areas, depending on the local leadership, it rivalled the authority of government officials. Its exclusive composition was lost when membership was opened to supporters of the National Revolution who had not been in the armed forces, and from 1942 its numbers declined, in keeping with the growing loss of public confidence in the whole of Vichy policy. At the same time the more active political elements within it were formed by Joseph Darnand into a smaller organization which eventually became the notorious Milice, a political police on the Nazi model. The contribution of this movement to the history of Vichy will be examined later, but its ascendancy marked the decline of the Légion as a whole. By 1943 large numbers of old members were hiding their framed diplomas, awarded for special services, and renouncing the oath of allegiance they had sworn to Pétain.

The only compulsory organization in Vichy France was for young men who would have been eligible for military service. Over 90,000 such men had been called up in June 1940 just before the war was lost, and those who were not taken prisoner often wandered aimlessly through the countryside in the wake of the defeat, vandalizing property, uncertain of where to report or what to do. For these Vichy set up a number of work camps in the countryside, called Chantiers de la Jeunesse, and for the next four years all young men reaching the age of twenty were liable to six or eight months in one of the camps. The man entrusted to organize and animate the Chantiers was General de la Porte du Theil, who had two successful careers behind him, first as army officer and second as scout leader for the Île de France. As Roger Austin (1983, p. 109) has shown, 'de la Porte du Theil believed that the scouting ideals of service to the community, loyalty, hardy initiative, and self-discipline could be combined to regenerate the nation through its young people.' With his flowing moustache and infectious energy he was said to resemble the warriors of ancient Gaul, and he deliberately used his image to press the ancestral merits of his organization. The propaganda posters superimposed a youth from the Chantiers dressed in green plus-fours, cloak and beret, on a flaxen-haired Gaul with helmet and double-headed axe.

This image suggested a military intention, but the Chantiers were much more an experiment in moral re-education and physical fitness. The first conscripts had to build their own camps in remote forest areas where food was scarce and comforts non-existent, and despite initial problems of poor morale and outbreaks of delinquency, the Chantiers survived to become an established feature of Vichy France. Road-mending, harvesting and the provision of wood and

27

charcoal were the main economic functions of the camps, all at a nominal wage level, and social integration of different classes was a major aim of the leaders though not entirely the experience of the youth involved. It was quintessential Vichy, a microcosm of the regime, and Pétain had few more devoted followers than General de la Porte du Theil.

The general's energy and idealism were shared by one of the non-military disciples of Pétain, the tennis champion Jean Borotra to whom Pétain entrusted a new Ministry of Sport. 'I lived only for my mission', he has said, and he, more than General de la Porte du Theil, saw the training he was offering to young people as a preparation for an ultimate military recovery of France. Both men tried to move the centre of youth education away from the classroom and into the open air, and for that reason their activities have been closely compared with the youth programmes of Fascist Italy and Nazi Germany. But they were not causally connected. If anything they derived more from the British public school ethic and the British emphasis on scouting and sport as builders of the whole personality, and Borotra himself was a fervent Anglophile.

There was a certain political naïvety about de la Porte du Theil and Jean Borotra, and there are many French people who remember their first acquaintance with the open air or with organized sport with gratitude, commending the enthusiasm of Vichy's youth leaders, and the vast increase in outdoor provisions. Both later claimed that their activities brought a new sense of community and purpose to French youth, but it was a youth increasingly defined to exclude the Jews, even though at first Jewish youth movements were allowed to continue, especially the Jewish scouting organization, which was deliberately excluded from the first Vichy ordinances reducing the Jews to second-class citizens. Almost every other aspect of Jewish life was affected, and by 1942 Vichy's claim to have constituted a new moral order through its education and youth policy stood side by side with its racialist record. They were twin aspects of a single system of nationalist values.

Within a fortnight of coming to power Vichy published the first decree against immigrant Jews. Those who had been naturalized as French in the years before the war were stripped of their rights. It was the first in a detailed series of measures by which the Jews became the official pariahs of the nation and were exposed to endless harrassment and eventually the threat or reality of deportation. The object was to make Vichy France a unitary nation along the lines of the motto 'France for the French' which had adorned the masthead of *l'Action Française* since the days of the Dreyfus affair. It was not a racial measure, claimed the regime, but a measure taken for reasons of state – but the definition in the statutes was a racial one, and Nazis in the occupied zone were pleasantly surprised to note that Vichy's first laws against the Jews were fully in line with their own. Vichy went on to set up a special commissariat to deal with Jewish affairs over which the Nationalist Xavier Vallat first presided, to be followed in 1942 by the fanatical racist Darquier de Pellepoix; and until recently it was often argued that Vallat was true to Vichy's limited conception of anti-semitism, while under Darquier Vichy lost control to the Nazis. However, in the light of much new evidence from the archives and the detailed study by Marrus and Paxton (1981), this distinction has been blurred, and Vichy throughout is seen to be responsible for racial discrimination against its own citizens, but even more so against stateless Jewish refugees who had come to France for asylum. The horrific deportations of these helpless people began in 1942, as will be seen in chapter 5.

Freemasons, communists and trade unionists were the other dark forces in Vichy's demonology. Ever since freemasonry in France had identified itself with rationalism, educational reform and anti-clericalism, it had been a declared public enemy of both the Catholic Church and right-wing politics. Condemned by the Pope in the late nineteenth century and labelled by Charles Maurras and the Action Française as the sinister influence behind republican politicians, the freemasons and their associations, known as lodges, came immediately under attack once the Vichy government was established. A series of decrees dissolved the lodges and exposed freemasons to dismissal from public office, particularly in the teaching profession. Even more instructions were issued to Vichy officials to hunt down communists of every description, and to produce endless lists of names and addresses of communist party members which soon came to clutter the archives of every prefecture. Local studies, like that of Pierre Laborie (1980) for the *département* of the Lot, show just how far anti-communism was the prime obsession of Vichy, and how communist conspiracies were seen behind every gesture of opposition to the regime; a close watch was kept on all previous militants of the party, and those thought to be most dangerous were either imprisoned or put on to the secret 'Liste S', which contained names of all those to be arrested immediately there was any threat to public order. When the Vichy police chief in the American film *Casablanca* (1943) reacts to any disturbance with the throw-away line 'Round up all the usual suspects', the fiction is closer to fact than the director Michael Curtiz probably realized.

The details of those on the 'Liste S' came mostly from pre-war activities of the individuals named, and trade unionism was not least among such activities retrospectively condemned as dangerous to the nation. In August 1940 all national trade union organizations were dissolved, though some unions at a local level were allowed to continue a brief, ineffectual existence until Vichy's labour legislation was completed. It is important to notice that employers' associations were also dissolved at the same time, testifying to Vichy's intention to attack the class struggle from both ends, and Pétain's speeches contained numerous denunciations of the rapacious nature of capitalism and the uncontrolled power of money. But this anti-capitalism was a moral position, not an economic or political one, and Vichy had no trace of socialism or collectivization in its doctrines. There was a moral commitment to bring workers and employers together in each business enterprise and to create an organic unity at the workplace, and the labour charter (*Charte du Travail*) of October 1941 was directed to that end. It made claims to inaugurate a new era in industrial relations, but since the organic structures were heavily weighted towards the owners, management and white-collar staff, it did no more than dress up a long-standing system of economic inequality in the tinsel of corporatism. It was the area of maximum unreality in Vichy's policies. The economic life of France was utterly dependent on the German occupation, and all Vichy was left to control were the ways in which labour and management organized themselves. The charter imposed few, if any, restrictions on management but it halted over fifty years of trade union development and repressed the authentic voices of labour.

The labour legislation was the last item in the National Revolution, and the edifice was theoretically complete. It relied heavily on a controlled press and radio to advertise its achievements, but the main agents of propaganda were the enthusiasts within the youth and veteran movements. Apart from the Légion and the Chantiers there were the voluntary Compagnons de France which initiated teenage boys into the discipline and service later demanded of them in the work camps, and the leadership school at Uriage near Grenoble which set out to train the 'natural' youth leaders in the art of revitalizing society, while within the ordinary schools, teachers were expected to orientate pupils towards the epic qualities of duty and sacrifice embodied in the figure of Pétain by comparing him to Joan of Arc, and by singing the national youth hymn, 'Maréchal, nous voilà'.

It is at this level that most people now remember the National Revolution, at the level of an ephemeral song which had a singable tune to offset its obsequious words. But in many ways Pétain's crusade caught some of the direction of the age; a greater provision for outdoor activities and sport, more concern for the welfare of old people, more family legislation, more state interference in the running of the economy, and a greater reliance on appointed experts rather than elected representatives. Where it failed totally was in its substantive aim to produce a new generation of lifetime believers in 'Travail, Famille, Patrie' as preached by the ideologues of Vichy. Whether it could have succeeded in more favourable conditions is not really at issue, for the National Revolution owed its opportunity to the conditions of defeat and occupation, and its success or failure was always dependent on those conditions.

From the start the constraints of occupation provoked a response from Vichy favouring negotiation with the occupiers, and this response soon bitterly divided the country. Gradually, as the divisions sharpened, it was increasingly realized that Vichy's *internal* policy was also divisive, precisely at the points where it claimed to be a unifying force. As more and more people became aware of this fact, the popularity of Pétain was affected, but for two years the mythic structure of Pétainism held up well, and popular discontent was directed primarily against the ministers thought to be misleading the Marshal. The separation familiar to historians of the *ancien régime* re-emerged. There was an absolute monarch who could do no wrong, and there were ministers behind the throne among whom evil flourished. Pierre Laval was seen to personify this archetypal role of evil counsellor, and the evil for which he was held responsible was the policy of collaboration. It is difficult to make further headway with the history of Vichy without folding in this vital ingredient.

3　Collaboration

Once the armistice had been signed and the Government at Vichy had launched the National Revolution, collaboration with Germany was seen by Pétain and Laval not as an option but as a necessity. The question was not whether there should be collaboration but in what direction and to what extent it should be pursued, and the major problem in 1940 was not how to persuade the French people to accept it, but how to persuade the German Government to agree to it.

To judge from the ease and frequency with which Marshal Pétain used the word 'collaboration' in the first months of Vichy it is obvious that he discerned no sinister overtones in the word. He used it to signify joint arrangements between occupiers and occupied which would facilitate the task Vichy had set itself in creating a new moral order. Pétain told the French that he had asked for an armistice because he believed it would limit the disaster of the defeat. After the armistice he saw it as a continuation of his role to try and limit the disasters of the occupation, including the appalling loss of one and a half million French soldiers to prisoner-of-war camps. If Germany was willing to collaborate then he saw it as his duty to prepare the ground for an eventual peace treaty. Once this was signed then he, Marshal Pétain would have extracted France from the worst catastrophe in its history. It could not be called a military victory like Verdun, but it would be the next best thing, a victory over disasters, a renaissance after the darkest hours, a phoenix out of the ashes. Collaboration was what he wanted, and to that end he made his own discreet attempts to get in touch with Hitler during August and September 1940. Only negotiations at the highest level could result in the kind of agreement he had in mind.

Pierre Laval also wanted collaboration but he had no view of himself as a spiritual leader like Pétain, leading the children of France out of bondage into a promised land. He had opposed the war as a criminal absurdity, and he now saw it as equally absurd to deny that Germany was supreme in continental Europe and would soon be overlord of Britain as well. Good sense in his view dictated that France should work out a form of collaboration which would give her the most favourable position possible within the new Europe. He believed that he alone could drive the necessary bargains to secure this position, and he was prepared to make concessions, confident that Germany would respond in kind, particularly while the campaign against Britain was pending. Laval criticized the negotiations at the armistice talks for not having used the remaining strengths which France possessed to achieve a better settlement. These strengths were primarily the navy and the French territories in Africa, and he believed the Germans could be made to pay more heavily for an assurance of their continued neutrality. With less discretion than Pétain but with a great deal more success, he opened every possible line of communication with the German authorities.

In reality neither the attitude of Laval to collaboration nor that of Pétain was quite so simple or straightforward. History is not purely the story of people's intentions or motivations. Important as they are, they operate within a context, and the history of Laval's and Pétain's collaboration is no exception. Pétain could not be the disinterested spiritual leader, nor Laval the disinterested negotiator, that they themselves later claimed to have been. Pressures which gave their collaboration a much more ambiguous meaning came from three main sources. Firstly the armistice itself had not been an obligation but a choice: it was probably inevitable that someone in French government circles would have called for a ceasefire in the way Pétain did, but Pétain himself had been under no obligation to do so. He was not even an active military participant in the war. He had been called in by Reynaud to strengthen the resolve of the French to keep fighting, and Reynaud himself favoured continuing the conflict from overseas. Other ministers tried to do that, notably Georges Mandel who had been appointed at the same time and for the same reason as Pétain. Together with an assorted group of politicians Mandel embarked on the *Massilia* from Bordeaux with the collective aim of continuing the government and the war from North Africa. A younger government official, General de Gaulle, Under-Secretary of State at the War Ministry, went in a more unpopular direction, to London. A number of other people, scattered throughout the country, were unable or unwilling to leave France but repudiated the armistice nevertheless. Pétain had made a choice, and once made the choice was a constraining factor in his later policy, for he had positioned himself firmly against those who had chosen otherwise. He later said, on 7 April 1941, in one of his sternest broadcasts: 'There are not several ways of being loyal to France'; and the fact that he had Mandel and the others arrested in Algeria, and that he fully endorsed a military court which condemned the absent General de Gaulle to death on 2 August 1940, suggests that he already held that view when he came to power. Pétain was committed to actions which would prove that staying in France, staying in government and negotiating with the victorious Germans were the only true ways of serving France. In collaboration he sought to justify his own choice, and he became more and more antagonistic to those who had decided to continue the war.

Secondly, the British attack on the French fleet at Mers-el-Kébir was a major influence on the spirit in which both Pétain and, still more, Laval conducted their negotiations with the Germans. It was not just that they expected an imminent British defeat at the hands of the Germans, but that after Mers-el-Kébir the potential defeat was viewed with indifference, if not even with a sense of satisfaction. Anti-British feeling at Vichy in July 1940 was a motivating force which cannot be overestimated.

Thirdly, the very nature of the authoritarian regime established on 10 July, and the similarity of many aspects of the National Revolution to ideas and practices which had thrived in all the dictatorships, from Salazar's Portugal to Hitler's Germany, gave the process of collaboration a political dimension, however neutral it might seem as a diplomatic necessity. The early actions of Vichy against Jews, freemasons, trade unionists and the various levels of left-wing political representation in the country laid the foundations of the new order in France at the same time as the negotiations with Abetz in Paris were moving towards a recognition of the new order in Europe. The two were acknowledged by Pétain to be closely linked. In his broadcast of 8 October which featured the concept of collaboration a full fortnight before he met Hitler, Pétain carefully spelt out the importance of a new kind of peace with Germany as an integral part of the National Revolution on which the Vichy regime was to be built. Read by Pétain, the speech was mainly written by Gaston Bergery whose political career in the 1930s had been aimed at bringing Left and Right together in a common front, and who was one among several politicians who came to Vichy to preach the merits of a fascist-style political structure over those of the traditional Right or the republican Left.

There was therefore, as Amouroux (1977) has convincingly argued, collaboration before Collaboration. The handshake of Hitler and Pétain at the little railway station of Montoire on 24 October 1940 was less the start of something new than a stage in a process which both Pétain and Laval had initiated from the earliest days of the Vichy regime, or even before. But that still leaves the question of what collaboration actually meant and how far it should be developed. The complications from this point are legion.

Returning from Montoire, Pétain and Laval faced an anxious circle of ministers, not all of whom had either been consulted or were in favour of such a major public display of Franco-German negotiations. Pétain stiffly assured them that only the principle of collaboration had been accepted by either side, and for him this meant only economic agreements, not military ones. This distinction was made even more sharply in a letter he sent to General Weygand, who had become increasingly critical of Laval's overtures to the Germans and who had been dismissed by Pétain as Minister of National Defence and sent on a military mission to North Africa. Weygand viewed Pétain's decision to shake hands with Hitler as a serious mistake, not least because of the support that Montoire elicited in pro-German circles.

Among the Nazi sympathizers and French fascist groups in Paris the meeting and the handshake were welcomed as a historic move towards a close integration of France in the Nazi New Order, and Pétain, who had been thought to be frustrating such a move, was roundly congratulated. Elsewhere the authorized press was suitably impressed by the event, but stressed its exploratory nature, while among the public at large there were the first major stirrings of revolt against the obedience which Pétain had demanded and received. Enough critical letters arrived at the Hôtel du Parc to make Pétain and his intimate advisers fully aware that his leadership was in dispute. His broadcast to the nation on 30 October, explaining Montoire, failed to re-establish his credibility among the doubters. He declared that he had chosen to see Hitler and had not been forced; he admitted that he had accepted the principle of collaboration; and he proclaimed that this collaboration was within the framework of the new European order. None of these points carried the reassurance he intended.

We can now see that Pétain had very little idea of what he was doing when he went to Montoire. The meeting had no agenda and there was no detailed exchange of points at issue. Pétain said little, and Hitler, once he realized that Pétain was not going to join Germany in a military agreement, lost interest and fell back on hollow generalities. Laval had been flattered by the unexpected opportunity of meeting Hitler and it appeared that Pétain responded in much the same way. The handshake was symptomatic, a gesture which gave the lead to official Franco-German encounters at all levels of the two administrations, but which was not the finalization of any hard-won agreement. It set the tone for future collaboration, and it constrained Pétain even more in his choice of policy, but it achieved nothing of substance. It must be ascribed to the delusions of grandeur that progressively undermined Pétain's judgement. He could not resist the temptation of the epic moment. 'It is I alone whom History will judge', he concluded at the end of his broadcast. It was one of his least prophetic statements, for with him he carried a considerable number of others. History was severe on them all.

This could not have been confidently foreseen in 1940. Laval's pragmatic claim that there were bargains still to be negotiated was sustained by the international situation right through to the winter of 1941–2. In the autumn of 1940, with the Battle of Britain still undecided, Laval's pragmatism seemed irrefutable at Vichy. But his methods were not those of any negotiator. He was more inventive and more active. When the Germans were unreceptive he set out to arouse their interests. When they became demanding he set out to anticipate them. Unlike most of his Vichy colleagues he not only had a list of things to protect, he also had a list of things to offer. Collaboration for Pétain was an end product, a harmonious relationship with Germany, preferably within the terms of a peace treaty. For Laval it was both an end and a means to that end; it was the day-to-day process of politics.

In that process Laval handed to the Germans the French shares in the Bohr copper mines in Yugoslavia, and authorized the transfer of the Belgian gold reserves into German hands. Neither action seemed to him a surrender of anything essential to French interests, but neither brought him any closer to the favoured position in Nazi Europe that he desired. Increasingly he kept his plans to himself, refusing to inform his ministerial colleagues, but he appointed an assistant to be on the spot in Paris for regular meetings with Abetz. That assistant was Fernand de Brinon, a journalist who had been the first to interview Hitler in 1933, a founder of the Franco-German Committee which worked during the 1930s for the close partnership of France and Nazi Germany and, through this committee, a close friend of Otto Abetz. He was obsequious, indiscreet and an open admirer of Nazism, and on 3 November Laval made him French Ambassador to the German Reich in Paris.

De Brinon served Laval well and stayed at his post throughout the occupation. From the start his collaboration was ideological, and it exceeded by far the agreements over food, prisoners of war, the demarcation line, and the mass of daily adjustments to the occupation sought by most Vichy officials. He was a French government appointment, unsolicited by the Germans, and as such must be seen as the Nazi end of the Vichy spectrum, and an index of the ideological preferences of Laval himself, although Laval liked to be seen as a hard-headed peasant from the Auvergne, closer to the local horse-traders than to the ideologues in right-wing political movements. Indeed, it was for his arrogance and stubbornness, not for his ideological preferences, that Laval was dismissed and arrested by Pétain on 13 December 1940. The Germans secured his release and tried to get him reinstated, raising every objection to his successor Pierre-Etienne Flandin. They closed the demarcation line and severely restricted all travel within the occupied zone. The head of the French navy, Admiral Darlan, was the only Vichy minister allowed as a go-between, and in February 1941 Pétain appointed him in Flandin's place with the explicit mission to improve Franco-German relations.

The choice of Darlan and the first few months of his appointment directed the eyes of France back to Mers-el-Kébir, to Fashoda and ultimately to the battle of Trafalgar in which Darlan's great-grandfather had been killed. Between April and June 1941 he almost took France into the war on the side of Germany and against Britain, not just out of vestigial Anglophobia, but in defence of Vichy's sovereignty over the French Empire. From London General de Gaulle had challenged that sovereignty as an integral part of his attack on the entire legitimacy of Vichy as the true government of France. Before he placed himself at the head of the Free French he offered to serve under a superior officer, General Noguès, who was in Algeria at the time of the armistice. Noguès remained staunchly loyal to Pétain, but in French West and Equatorial Africa de Gaulle's challenge was upheld, and in July and August the French territories of the Chad, the Ivory Coast, the Cameroons, the Congo and Oubangui-Chari all declared for de Gaulle against Pétain, as did several French colonies outside Africa, notably the New Hebrides, Tahiti and New Caledonia and the important settlements in Indo-China under the Governor-Generalship of General Catroux. The more affluent and socially conservative settler population of Senegal in West Africa remained Pétainist, and became even more loyal to Vichy when de Gaulle's small company of Free French forces launched an attack on the Senegalese port of Dakar on 23 September, aided by the British navy. The attack was a disaster, and Churchill called it off after two days, leaving the Vichy press exultant at having repulsed what Pétain called 'the forces of dissidence'. From the perspective of Vichy as the government of France, voted in by a huge majority only two months before, the attack on Dakar was treasonous, and the aid given by Britain no less perfidious than

37

Mers-el-Kébir. Darlan's reaction to both as naval commander was a sense of personal outrage, which informed the whole of his policy when he was brought to the centre of the Vichy stage in 1941. He had favoured the idea of retaliatory bombing raids on Gibraltar after Mers-el-Kébir, and in May 1941, when Hitler asked him for permission to use air bases in Syria for his operations against Britain in Iraq, Darlan agreed. General Dentz, the French military governor in Syria, was instructed to co-operate, and a major shift in the meaning of collaboration took place. Darlan travelled not to a small French country town to meet Hitler, but to the Führer's retreat at Berchtesgaden, and when Gaullist and British forces attacked the troops of the unrepentant General Dentz in Syria, Darlan stood on the verge of declaring a co-belligerent status with Germany in the Middle East. Protocols to that effect were drawn up in Paris at the end of May, and Darlan brought them to Vichy for ratification. They were duly discussed. Weygand came over from Algeria to denounce them and issued what amounted to a threat of resignation, which hinted that North Africa might go over to the dissidents. Pétain, however, repeated his promise that there would be no military collaboration, and the protocols were never ratified. Vichy France did not declare war on Britain.

Several times in 1940 Hitler had asked Vichy to make bases available to German forces in French territories overseas, and Darlan's agreement was the first positive response. Yet Hitler showed no interest in translating a circumstantial agreement into a permanent one, and gave little backing to the efforts of Abetz in Paris to seize the Syrian opportunity for a full Franco-German partnership. At Montoire Hitler had rapidly cooled in his attitude to Pétain, and although the armistice held out a provision for a return of the French government to Paris, Hitler was not in favour of even that small recognition of French revival. Later, when French fascist sympathizers volunteered for the Eastern front to fight against communism, he refused to allow them any status as partners in the war, and they were ordered to fight in Nazi uniforms with only a small insignia specifying their country of origin. Had his vision of Europe involved a more equal role for France or even a more receptive estimation of French culture and traditions, it is difficult to see how he would have allowed Darlan's readiness for a military agreement to have foundered in the hesitations and reluctance of his ministerial colleagues. But by the climax of the Syrian affair Hitler had lost his enthusiasm for the Middle East. He was completing his plans for the invasion of Russia and the Syrian episode was relegated by Hitler's new initiative to the footnotes of military history.

In the event, Vichy lost Syria and Darlan made a tactical retreat within the southern zone, maintaining that he had a long list of German concessions which he would have demanded as a condition of military collaboration. Neither these, nor the details of how close he came to taking France into war, were known to the public, but the broadcasts of both Darlan and Pétain had alerted the French to a new stage in Franco-German relations, and the widespread reaction was to add Darlan to Laval as the malevolent and devious forces operating behind the Marshal's back. Darlan was felt to be even less approachable than Laval, less sympathetic to ordinary people's day-to-day problems, and less astute as a politician, and his unpopularity showed at public occasions. Pétain is said to have drawn attention to this when he heard a few shouts of 'Vive Darlan' intermingled with the rapturous applause given to himself on one of his urban tours. Turning to Darlan he said: 'I'd no idea you were a ventriloquist.'

There was little enough humour in Vichy by the end of 1941. With the invasion of Russia a new chapter of German demands on France brought an end to easy illusions of favoured positions in a New Europe or hopes of an imminent peace. By 1942 most of the French Empire, with the continued exception of Algeria, had become Gaullist, America had joined the war and withdrawn its tolerance of Vichy, the German armies were embedded in the protracted Russian campaign, and inside France both the zones were nurturing a growing number of resistance groups with mounting public support. There was now a new word in the French language, 'les collabos', used in every clandestine publication to designate those who negotiated with the Germans as traitors. Prefects' reports begin to shower the Vichy ministers with evidence that 'the road of collaboration' on which Pétain had embarked at Montoire was neither popular nor credible. They pleaded with the Ministry of Information to improve its propaganda. 'The policies of the Government' reported the prefect of the Tarn, 'are unfortunately widely misunderstood and no longer carry any conviction.' It was a typical summary of the way in which Franco-German relations were viewed as France entered the second full year of occupation.

Forced onto the defensive in its foreign, if not in its domestic, policy, Vichy trimmed its expectations accordingly, but if anything intensified its collaboration. The German offensive against Russia gave an ideological momentum to the war which fully coincided with Vichy's own political values, and anti-communism became not just an official persecution but a moral crusade. Even the 'decadence of the Third Republic' was surpassed by the 'barbarity of communism' and the hunt for communists within France became the main duty of the Vichy police. It also became the excuse for collaboration in the first war crimes to be perpetrated by the Germans in the occupied zone. The crimes, the mass shooting of hostages, were not unprovoked, in the sense that a German officer was assassinated in Paris in September 1941 and two more in Nantes and Bordeaux in October. But the Germans far exceeded the conventions of war by taking reprisals against innocent civilians who were in no way implicated in the assassinations, and Vichy, through its Minister of the Interior, Pierre Pucheu, collaborated by choosing a number of communists as the hostages who would be shot, and rigging the law to make them retrospectively guilty of crimes punishable by death. Pucheu's use of a Special Service in the Paris judiciary to carry through this violation of justice and human decency was dictated by a growing determination in the French government to salvage the declining status of Vichy with a display of resolute activity as soon as public order was threatened. It became policy for Vichy ministers to fulfil the letter of the armistice by asserting French independent action whenever the Germans threatened to interfere and take the law into their own hands. If this meant carrying out the choosing of hostages, the arrest of resisters, the recruitment of labour for Germany, or eventually the deportation of Jews, then Vichy believed it was better for French sovereignty if these acts were carried out by French officials rather than German. It was the beginning of the 'shield' philosophy of collaboration, the claim made both before and after the Liberation by Pétain and Laval that action by Vichy had shielded the French people from far greater repression at the hands of the Germans. By extension it became the major argument for Vichy's whole existence.

It was in defence of this 'shield' philosophy that Laval returned to power in April 1942, and Pétain decided to remain as head of state even when the Germans occupied the Vichy zone in the following November. But it was a long way from the optimistic meaning that Vichy had given to collaboration in 1940. By 1942 it was clear that the mutual benefits hoped for at Montoire had not arrived, and that collaboration was a one-way activity. As such it could only be openly justified for its negative value, as a policy to *éviter le pire*, to prevent an unspecified fate at the unrestrained hands of the occupiers. How Laval pursued this new policy will be discussed in chapter 5. What it achieved for Vichy was to keep its concept of collaboration at arm's length from that of the Nazi sympathizers in Paris, even if the difference in practice was often far less easy to distinguish.

Historians have now endorsed the distinction between Vichy's collaboration and that of the French fascists by using the term *collaborationism* to describe the committed, ideological identification with Nazi Germany for which the Paris-based fascists fought and struggled before, during and after the occupation. While this is a useful linguistic solution to problems of categorization it should not obscure the very considerable inter-relationship between Vichy and the fascist collaborators. De Brinon, Laval's man in Paris, was certainly a collaborationist. Two of Darlan's ministers, Paul Marion at the Ministry of Information and Pierre Pucheu at the Ministry of Interior, had belonged in the 1930s to Jacques Doriot's Parti Populaire Français (PPF), which continued under the occupation to be the most successful of the fascist movements. Doriot himself, while rejected by Laval as a potential minister in 1940, nevertheless proclaimed himself as 'l'homme du Maréchal', and for over a year publicized Pétain as the providential hero, and used Pétain's meeting with Hitler at Montoire as justification from the very highest authority for a close collaboration with Germany. The other major leader of Paris collaborationism, Marcel Déat, was valued by Abetz and Laval during their first negotiations in the autumn of 1940, and became so identified with Laval that Pétain had him arrested alongside Laval in December. Eventually Laval brought Déat into the French government in March 1944, after several months of pressure from the Gestapo head Oberg and from Otto Abetz, but during the years which separated their relationship in 1940 and the appointment of 1944, Laval and Déat were frequently involved in mutual projects. They were together on 28 August 1941 at the launch of the Légion des Volontaires Français contre le Bolchévisme (LVF), which was formed to fight on the Eastern front in defence of 'Christian Virtue' against 'Communist Barbarism'. In fact, by coincidence, they were both injured at that meeting by bullets from the revolver of Paul Collette, a young right-wing nationalist who was opposed to collaboration and who set out to assassinate Laval. In November 1941 Pétain signed a letter to the LVF in which he responded to the Légion's expressions of fidelity with the warmest commendation of their 'crusade, led by Germany' which would contribute to the fight against the Bolshevik peril and thereby protect France and fulfil 'the hopes of a reconciled Europe'. Doriot, who went with the first detachment of the LVF, published the letter in his newspaper *le Cri du Peuple* and although Pétain later said he had signed the letter without reading it, and that the substance was composed by de Brinon, the identification of the Marshal with the ideals of French volunteers fighting in German uniform was publicly apparent. Furthermore the chancellor of the Académie Française,

Abel Bonnard, patronized the concept and organization of the LVF and in April 1942 he became Vichy's Minister of Education.

By comparing the Vichy and the Paris press it is clear that their propaganda was different in both style and content, but in 1943–4 Philippe Henriot, the Vichy Minister of Propaganda at the time, began his regular broadcasts for Vichy radio which became the most effective collaborationist propaganda of the whole occupation. Reaching the small towns and country areas of the south which were untouched by the ideas and politics of a Doriot or a Déat, he instilled a level of acute anxiety among people who were not yet fully committed to the Resistance by his skilful insinuations that their farms, their homes, their food, their children, were prey to an all-consuming communism. After Henriot's assassination at the end of June 1944, the potent voice of collaborationism was still to be heard on Vichy radio in the populist, caustic and often amusing presentation of news by Jean-Hérold Paquis, who throughout 1941 had been Vichy's radio commentator on the provincial tours of Pétain, and was a member of the PPF.

These relationships across the two zones, and across the worlds of Vichy traditionalism and fascist radicalism, were never the norm, but were significant in so far as they were the overt links which covered a more impenetrable world of police and intelligence networks. Recruits to the LVF, for example, were felt to be more useful to Vichy inside France than on the Eastern front and they were extensively used in the internal crusade against communism; and in 1943–4 the Vichy drive against resisters by its own police benefited in particular areas from the information and eventually armed support provided by the para-military wing of the PPF, by members of the normally more quiescent group 'Collaboration', as well as from the Milice which had its fascist origins not in Paris but in Vichy. Its leader, Joseph Darnand, was the most conspicuous collaborationist outside Paris and he, like Henriot, was a full minister at Vichy from December 1943, placed in charge of all the internal forces of law and order. At that late date, an increasingly powerless Pétain, detached by moments of senility as well as by growing uncertainty about his own and Vichy's raison d'être, nevertheless approved of Darnand as a loyal and heroic soldier from both wars. He was less enthusiastic about Henriot, and totally opposed to Déat.

No history of collaboration can be adequately written without an exploration of this fascist temptation to which Vichy partially succumbed. Laval is a key figure in this respect because he not only formed many of the links himself, but also repudiated and rejected many more. He, more than anyone, was responsible for convincing Abetz that Doriot and the other fascist leaders like Bucard and Deloncle would be a disaster for Franco-German relations if they were allowed into power. This was Hitler's view as well, and Abetz became the main source of fascist frustration in Paris. He distributed favours and money: he helped Déat build his own movement, the Rassemblement National Populaire (RNP) in 1941 and he encouraged the LVF; but what he gave with one hand he withheld with the other, and his initiatives produced fragmentation and jealousies within the fascist groups and among their self-projecting leaders. The legacy of the splits and rivalries of the fascist leagues in the 1930s was not the only reason why there was no coherent movement of collaborationism in occupied France. Hitler saw them as potentially popular movements which might come to lead a rejuvenated nationalism as Nazism had done in Germany, and his instructions to Abetz were to divide and rule. Vichy traditionalists were alienated by the apparent social radicalism of the groups, by their raucous attacks on the military and clerical establishment, and by their unmitigated pro-Germanism, and Vichy officials blocked, diverted and restrained the activity of the fascist groups at all levels. Laval, the man most in the middle, was an operator and a negotiator. He would, and did, use the enthusiasm of the fascists and he shared their anti-communism, but his collaboration was never unqualified in the way that the Paris groups demanded. Doriot particularly attacked him, and Laval's response was to intensify his own control over all mechanisms of collaboration. Ironically, in what might well be called a fascist Europe, the most fascist elements in French society were kept away from positions of power, but then Hitler's Europe was never fascist in the way the French groups wanted any more than it was a new experiment in partnership in ways envisaged by Abetz, Laval or Pétain.

Divided and restricted, the collaborationists nevertheless paraded their wares with fascist style and ceremony. They were no longer on the illegal sidelines of republican France. At Maxims and La Tour d'Argent they ate the best meals with the heads of the German occupation; they published newspapers which were printed in hundreds of thousands; they wore Nazi uniforms, held public rallies and had easy access to the inner rooms of the Gestapo; they could travel and buy indiscriminately on the black market; they planted bombs outside synagogues and they victimized Jews in the literary world, theatre and cinema. From whatever vantage point assured by German patronage they looked on Paris as their own.

At their height in 1941–3 they numbered approximately 150,000, including strong outposts of the PPF in Marseille and Algeria, and branches of the PPF, 'Collaboration' and the 'Francistes' in most big towns, unlike Déat's RNP which was based almost exclusively in Paris and the occupied zone. Doriot, the forceful street orator, man of the people, ex-communist, and activist in all anti-communist movements since 1935, had nothing in common with the intellectual ascetic, journalist-politician, Marcel Déat. Doriot was contemptuous of Laval and Déat for having been ministers in the Third Republic – a republic which had dismissed him as mayor of the working-class suburb of St Denis. He intended the PPF as a popular fascist strike force against the political establishment, and appeared at one stage to be inciting the LVF into a Mussolini-style march on Vichy, though not on Pétain. Déat, by contrast, envisaged a single national-socialist party to cleanse Vichy of the militarists, monarchists and clericals epitomized by Pétain, to destroy the capitalist trusts and construct state socialism and a planned economy. Both leaders controlled forces numbering between 20–30,000, and they came together only briefly in forming the LVF when, in the frenzied excitement of the German invasion of Russia, they promised Hitler a volunteer force of 80,000. Numerous recruiting centres were set up and the pay promised to the volunteers was attractively high. It was August 1941 and Germany looked like defeating Russia within weeks. Everything was in favour of the recruitment, but to the consternation of the collaborationists and Abetz only 5,000 volunteers came forward, a mixture of mercenaries and idealists. A vigorous German medical examination eliminated over half as unfit for the harsh life on the Eastern front, and when Doriot left France with the first contingent they numbered under 1,000. Eventually in three years of service just under 6,000 Frenchmen fought in German uniform either for the LVF or in units of the Waffen SS, and most of them died in the fighting in freezing conditions outside Moscow in the winter of 1941-2 or in the various stages of the German retreat when they found themselves thrown into the guerrilla war against Russian partisans. Some of those who picked their way back to France through the debris of Hitler's Europe have persuaded certain historians that their cause was an honourable and heroic one. Courageous they may have been in an atrocious war, but courage is not all one asks of people who make major ideological gestures.

The fascist idealism of the LVF reflected in action the intellectual ideas which emanated from what Lucien Rebatet, the fascist sympathizer, writer and critic, called the 'Academy of Collaboration'. In daily newspapers, weeklies and cultural periodicals, the intellectual sympathizers with Nazism stimulated the activists with evocations of fascist vitality and youthfulness (Robert Brasillach), a Nietzschean transvaluation (Pierre Drieu la Rochelle) or the apocalyptic greatness of Hitler (Alphonse de Châteaubriant). From Louis-Ferdinand Céline came letters to the collaborationist press extending the cynical, fanatical ravings of his pre-war antisemitism, and from Rebatet, who described himself as 'Wagnerian, Nietzschean, antisemite and anticlerical, knowing by heart the folklore of national socialism', came an all-pervading spirit of nihilistic revolt. Not all these intellectuals stayed with collaborationism to the end: they were subject to paralysing disillusionment and despair in the same measure as illusions of greatness and fantasies of power, and Drieu tried suicide several times before he finally succeeded in 1945. But in the high days of collaborationism, they provided a visionary philosophy of a new age, which heralded the imminence of 'fascist man', and they offered a language of cultured extravagance in which to clothe the naked persecution of the Jews. For four years, wrote Brasillach (1955, p. 254), certain Frenchmen 'slept with Germany. They had quarrels, but the memory of the experience remains sweet'.

Collaboration and collaborationism were two points on an unbroken but complex continuum, as many Vichy officials discovered once the southern zone was fully occupied, and the German presence in the Roman arena of Nîmes promised as much to local fascists as it had done on the banks of the Seine. The prefect of the Gard, Chiappe, brother of the Paris Prefect of Police who had sympathized with fascist leagues in the 1930s, saw it as his duty to protect the population from the rigours of the occupation by treating the German military authorities in Nîmes as guests, not as occupiers. He showed them round Provence, invited them regularly to dinner, and slipped from the 'tactical shield' philosophy of collaboration into collaborationism, ending as a convinced patron of the local Milice. From a justification of necessity, his collaboration became an ideological choice. How far was he typical of Vichy in its last two years? This can only be answered when the alternatives to collaboration have been examined, alternatives which progressively forced the collaborators to redefine their aims and their methods. One of the alternatives was known as 'attentisme', a waiting on events and doing nothing of any substance in any direction, and many in the Vichy regime can be seen as 'attentistes'. The other alternative was Resistance.

4 Resistance

On 14 July 1940 there was no festive celebration of the fall of the Bastille. Pétain proclaimed it as a day of mourning for the defeat of France, and, coming four days after the vote of full powers to the Marshal, there was no attempt to question his decision. But by 11 November, the anniversary of victory over Germany in the First World War, the situation had already begun to change. Pétain was still the object of worship and veneration, but he had shaken hands with Hitler at Montoire, and for small numbers of people scattered throughout France this was seen as a flagrant capitulation to the enemy, even more unacceptable than the armistice itself.

At 5.30 in the afternoon of 11 November students from the Sorbonne and pupils from the Paris Lycées assembled at the Arc de Triomphe and attempted to lay the traditional wreaths at the tomb of the unknown soldier. For several weeks there had been isolated student protests in the Latin Quarter – particularly when the physicist, Paul Langevin, was arrested by the Germans – while during early November the first widely heard broadcasts from the BBC called for a demonstration at all war memorials on the 11th. At the Arc de Triomphe the French police were first on the scene and broke up the small crowd with baton charges, but they were followed by a brutal show of military strength by the occupying forces who cleared the area with bursts of machine-gun fire. Rumours reached all parts of the capital that tens of students and schoolchildren had been killed, but even the much reduced reality of several wounded and over 100 arrested was a break in the uneasy calm which had settled over France since the events of June. It was one of the first moments of resistance, but it did not set a model for resistance activity throughout France. Apart from an impressive strike by miners in the north-east in May 1941 in which both employers and the occupying forces were openly defied by the collective strength of workers and local communist leaders, there were very few public confrontations with the Germans in the two years after the defeat. Early resistance was almost entirely a matter of secret initiatives by

46

individuals and small groups, who made up only a very small percentage of the population.

Most French people reacted to the hopelessness of the situation by keeping to their daily lives, grudgingly coming to terms with the occupation, harbouring increasing resentment towards the Germans but leaving the war to those who were obviously still involved. France could no longer be seen as an active belligerent nor, within Vichy's codes of collaboration, as even a passive one. The arguments of common sense and practicality buttressed not only Pétainism but also inaction. Few people saw any way in which the French could continue a war which had been so comprehensively lost. This did not mean that they wanted the Germans to win, or to stay in France. Quite the contrary. But it did mean that their priorities for survival lay in outwitting not the German army but what the Bretons call 'la chienne du monde' – the malevolent beast of poverty, hunger and personal or family disaster.

In this context, those who refused to accept that the war had been lost were unusually obstinate. The refusal flew in the face of all considered opinion. It was, in the words of the writer and resister, Jean Cassou, 'un refus absurde', and its 'absurdity' marked the early resisters as rebels in the eyes of Vichy, as eccentrics within their local society and as dreamers among themselves.

The dream image is one of the most constant in the recollections of the period. Resisters often remember 1940–1 as a kind of waking dream; they talk of searching blindly in the night, of outstretched fingertips groping for contact, and dreamlike visions of adventurous operations which far outran the sober calculations of their rational selves. The most basic account of early resistance shows an amazing number of grand designs projected by individuals quite unconnected with each other, and such designs contained the seeds of almost all future resistance, theory and practice alike.

Symptomatic of these grandiose dreams were the extravagant hopes of General de Gaulle in London. On 18 June he was allowed by Churchill to broadcast to all French forces to continue the war by joining him in London, and in retrospect that famous appeal is given a logical place in the unfolding history of Gaullist power. But all those who took part in the early days of the Free French movement in London stress the extraordinary position of de Gaulle at the time. Aged 50, he was young by comparison with most of the French Army command, and his rank was only that of a provisional general. He had had a brief experience of working for Prime Minister Reynaud, he was an expert on mobility in warfare, but he was utterly naïve in the field of party politics. Yet here he was apparently challenging

Marshal Pétain as the authentic voice of France. Even to many of the French who found themselves in London at the time, his broadcasts seemed impossibly pretentious, while to people in France his first period of resistance was hardly more than a curious, tantalizing piece of unsubstantiated news. Only for a few was it a meaningful call to action. But without his initial vision, and without his apparently 'absurd' hopes of diverting loyalties from Pétain to himself, de Gaulle would probably have made little or no impact on either the French or the British scene.

De Gaulle's was a pioneer voice of revolt, made national and international by the BBC. Other rebellious voices did not have a similar medium at their disposal, but their early stand against submission to defeat and occupation were no less pioneering at a local level. De Gaulle's broadcast was only one of several starting points for French resistance, and it was not until late in 1941 that he himself had any idea how many other initiatives had been taken just as early as his own. Similarly, many of the pioneers of revolt *inside* France in the first six months after the defeat were unaware of each other's existence, and often knew nothing of de Gaulle's initiative in London. The image of a dream world is apt because it accurately suggests not only illusions but also the kind of disconnected actions which characterize a dream and which were very much the reality of resistance in 1940–1.

In Brive-la-Gaillarde, in the centre of France, the day before de Gaulle launched his appeal in London, Edmond Michelet typed an appeal to the local people not to surrender. As a Catholic Democrat, and organizer of voluntary social welfare and education in the town, he was sufficiently well known locally for his opinion to affect many others, and he became the centre of a small group openly assertive of the need to stand firm against any compromise with the invaders. Resolute defiance followed independently from officers General Cochet and Captain Frenay, from university teachers and intellectuals François de Menthon in Savoie, Pierre-Henri Teitgen in Montpellier, Jean Cassou and Paul Rivet in Paris, from working-class communists Charles Tillon in Bordeaux, Georges Guingouin in Limoges, Joseph Pastor in Marseille and Auguste Lecoeur in the Nord, from socialist schoolmaster Martial Brigouleix in the small town of Tulle in the Corrèze, from the Dominican priest Père Maydieu, escaping from a prisoner-of-war camp at Orléans, and from Jesuits Père Fessard and Chaillet in Lyon. It came from women no less than men, from Bertie Albrecht, who was engaged in voluntary service in the southern zone, Lucie Aubrac, a schoolteacher in Lyon, Marie-Madeleine Fourcade who had moved from Paris to help run a youth centre in Vichy, Agnès Humbert at the Musée des Arts et Traditions populaires in Paris . . . It is invidious to stop the list of names at this point.

Some of these individuals became household names in French Resistance history, others remained celebrated at a local level only. They came from a wide variety of occupations and from a wide variety of places. For a multitude of reasons they made an individual stand against inaction and subservience and created groups of like-minded friends and contacts which eventually became the well-known movements of Resistance and networks of intelligence and escape.

In the occupied zone the movements were small and precarious due to the constant presence of the Germans, but the networks had a more obvious rationale than similar ventures in the south. The major movements to survive the initial disasters of inexperience and German infiltration became known as 'Organisation civile et militaire', 'Libération-Nord', 'Ceux de la Libération' and 'Ceux de la Résistance', all working through clandestine pamphlets or news-papers to build up a solidarity of attitudes and disparate actions which could be as small as turning round a signpost to infuriate a convoy of Germans ('narguer les Allemands') or as large as the distribution of thousands of tracts. Some also made the first tentative steps towards the hiding of arms and the planning of sabotage. The networks were more concentrated in their aims and gradually became linked either to the Free French in London, or the British intelligence service and the Special Operations Executive (SOE) set up by Britain to undermine Nazi-occupied Europe with specially trained agents. These networks in the north were dominated by two, the 'Confrérie Notre-Dame' and 'Alliance', but there were others like 'Alibi' or 'Agir', and eventually 'Prosper'. Unlike the movements, none of these networks declared their existence through clandestine publications. To the vast majority of the French they remained totally unknown until after the war.

In the unoccupied zone, movements were created just as early as in the north and west, but they had a more expansive character and the degree of discussion and the level of information in their underground publications reflected the comparative absence of sudden decimating raids by the authorities. Three major movements particular to the zone, 'Combat', 'Libération-Sud' and 'Franc-Tireur', were flanked by sparsely developed networks which dealt far more with escape routes than with espionage, while across both zones from May 1941 developed the only major movement common to both, the 'Front National' organized by communists but open to all.

The obvious question which dominated the first meeting of friends, colleagues or party activists was 'What could be done?' It was a question which had entitled numerous political tracts in the history of revolt from Chernyshevsky to Lenin, but very few early resisters looked to theory for their 'point de départ'. There was little, if any, theoretical guidance to be had. There were remote historical antecedents in the guerrilla actions of the Spanish people in the peninsular war against Napoleon, there were more recent examples of individual actions in the fight against dictatorship in Italy, Germany and Spain, and there was a long tradition of pride in the patriotism of revolt from the volunteers of Year II in the French Revolution to the stand of the Communards against the Prussians in 1871. But essentially the history of resistance had to be created. It was not inherited, and was available as part of recent folklore only as a barricade tradition in which the cobblestones of Paris seemed historically numbered to be taken up periodically for the defence of popular justice and freedom. But no barricades were to be erected until 1944. Until then the average resister made more use of ruse and guile than of the heroic stance of Delacroix's 'Liberté guidant le peuple' of 1830. And information was as precious as arms.

Gradually, after the pioneering moves of individuals, the motivation to resist became more closely linked with the effects of the occupation and Vichy legislation. The lingering effects of the *exode* and the continued dislocation of thousands of people unable or unwilling to return to their homes accentuated the human problems of the period; it also led to the early formation of groups of 'exiles' – whether from Alsace-Lorraine, from Paris, or from occupied countries outside France – determined to find ways of staying together and opposing the Nazi domination of Europe. The deprivation and shortages were selectively felt by French people; they were also selectively important in creating a mood of protest and revolt among the working classes and the poorer sections of society. Progressively the German requisitions in the countryside alienated the peasantry and although alienation did not inevitably translate itself into resistance, it increasingly meant that resisters and people on the run could be harboured with a degree of safety in the woods and hills of rural France. The censorship and enforced propaganda of the Germans affected all journalists, writers and teachers in varying ways, and the mere process of continuing to report, write and teach openly could be a first step in confrontation with the occupiers. The continued pursuit of trade union demands at work, whether for better pay and conditions, or freedom to meet and organize, had similar results among workers whose unions had been abolished.

In the Vichy zone in particular many were propelled into opposition by political victimization. Socialists who were removed from local councils, communists who were arrested for any sign of continued political activity, freemasòns who were denounced and sacked from their jobs, Jews who were made into second-class citizens or worse, working women who were constrained to leave their jobs, all were faced by Vichy with the choice of submission or some form of rebellion. The path to resistance was far from the obvious one to many of the victimized, but after the meeting of Pétain with Hitler at Montoire, and still more after the closer collaboration of Darlan with the war aims of Germany in the Middle East and in Russia, the link between political protest against Vichy and resistance against the Germans became increasingly marked.

With such a diversity of origins resistance could never have been a purely military reaction, or one limited to those with a leaning towards espionage. From the start, resistance had a role and justification in the lives of many people who had no ambition to hold a gun, or memorize a coded message, though as the occupation grew in its violence the pressure on the French people to defend themselves by force intensified, and the military nature of resistance came to predominate. To do justice to the diversity of motives and the variables of situation, and to the changing dynamic of the period, requires a subtlety and sense of relativism which generalities cannot possess. All history should be the history of ordinary people as well as national or international leaders, so the history of the Resistance is no different in kind. But when leadership was such a local phenomenon as it was in the Resistance, and when almost all the movements grew painfully from below rather than being established from above, the historian who goes into the provincial towns and villages of France in pursuit of Resistance history is responding to the basic nature of the event. A good sense of location was invaluable to resisters: a set of local maps is now essential for the historian.

The towns were all-important at the beginning. Later the focus rests in equal measure on parts of the countryside. In the southern towns a café, a school or a library was often the place where groups first met to discuss the events. In 1940–1 such discussions attracted little notice from the Vichy police. Until the economy had been adjusted to the occupation, there were knots of unemployed or displaced people meeting in every community round a table or under a fountain in the main square. By 1942 such scenes were a rarity and by 1944 they had disappeared completely, whereas in the occupied zone it was dangerous to meet as a group from the beginning. Some Paris communists who were induced by the party's controversial neutrality before June 1941 to come into the open paid a heavy price for their indiscretion. Gabriel Péri, the party's leading anti-Nazi journalist before the Nazi-Soviet pact, and one of the party's inner committee who was most disturbed by the effects of the pact, was easily followed and arrested in Paris in May 1941. He was executed as a hostage six months later.

A series of meetings often came to nothing. But where the means existed, the first discussions were often followed by the production and distribution of a simple tract or the launch of a more ambitious bulletin or embryonic newspaper. The commitment which this involved was a decisive step in moving from attitudes to action, and the process of distribution necessitated new contacts and wider liaisons. The ripples of revolt began to spread. Producing a newspaper was a well-established political reflex in France, and should not be seen as an avoidance of more effective action. Hawking a newspaper round the streets had always been a political apprenticeship for marginal, or oppositional, groups. It was now a means of creating and sustaining new groups of activists, and having to do it secretly meant that increasing numbers of recruits were rapidly introduced to the problems and risks of clandestine activity.

The larger towns of France all contained a number of small printers, but there had also been a pre-war expansion in the market for typewriters and duplicators. This enabled early resisters to locate the simple mechanisms for reproducing basic tracts, but by 1942 duplicating ink and paper had become scarce and there was a much larger quantity of Resistance material to be circulated. Consequently more and more printers were pulled into the Resistance to produce typeset newspapers. The risks they ran were prodigious, and it is still a major source of professional pride for local printers to point to the cellars in which the clandestine press escaped detection.

The internal geography of the towns was a vital factor in the success or failure of such clandestine operations. The artisan area of Lyon, the Croix Rousse, was a labyrinth of steps, alleyways and interconnected houses which allowed people to disappear into a house at one level and emerge from a totally different house lower down, and the medieval *ruelles* of the towns in the south, Montpellier, Marseille and Toulouse, swallowed an escaping figure with ease.

The three main Resistance movements in the southern zone become known by the name of their newspapers, *Combat*, *Franc-Tireur* and *Libération* (sud), all published in Lyon, and in the occupied zone the same was true of the Paris-based movements *Libération* (nord), unrelated to its synonym in the south, and *Défense de la France*. The Front National had been launched in the clandestine pages of

L'Humanité, the central organ of the Communist party, and from Lyon came *Témoignage Chrétien*, long articles on the evils of Nazism and antisemitism written by Catholics and Protestants, whose distribution network virtually constituted a movement of its own.

It was in Paris that the first paper to use the title *Résistance* was launched, but the consequences for the intellectual group centred on the Musée de l'Homme was an indication of the special nature of German intelligence in the capital. In January 1941, only a month after the first appearance of the paper, the arrests began, and they continued remorselessly throughout the year, leading to several executions and numerous deportations.

Other early publications took the form of open letters to the French people and bore the stamp of a single person's determination to resist. Jean Texcier, a civil servant in the Ministry of Commerce, wrote what is normally seen as the first clandestine pamphlet, *Conseils à l'occupé*, in July 1940, and in November heard one of his subsequent letters quoted by Maurice Schumann on the BBC. More widely known in the south were a series of tracts called *Tour d'Horizon* from the pen of General Cochet of the French air force, who combined strong anti-Germanism with an equally strong Pétainism, a mixture which was far from unusual in 1940–1 when hopes that Pétain would outmanoeuvre the occupiers led many into the conviction that he was secretly working with the British. It turned out to be the wildest of all illusions in this period, but its prevalence helps to explain why both the leader of Vichy and his government were slow to be identified by the Resistance press as an enemy of equal stature to the German occupiers.

All publications, by groups or by individuals, in the first two years after the defeat were comparatively small and isolated events in the wider context of the occupation. But they *were* events, with the effect of crystallizing attitudes and creating structures. Their contents did not in every case set out an alternative course of action for citizens to follow, but they did, in every case, set out alternative information, which was not available to the French people through the official Vichy press and radio. By 1942 the Vichy media and the clandestine press made up two completely separate and contradictory sources of information, with the German media in the occupied zone constituting a third, and the BBC gaining an increasingly dominant position as the fourth. When the Germans occupied the southern zone in November 1942, considerable numbers of people were exposed to all four, and to these were added a regular listening to the Swiss radio, and eventually tracts and leaflets dropped by the British air force. Some radios could also be tuned to

Radio Moscow, or to de Gaulle's transmitters first in Brazzaville and later in Algiers.

As the extent of these alternatives became known to the Germans and to Vichy, their policy of suppression and persecution made sure that the choice of media became a dynamic element in the growth of resistance. There were 'armchair resisters' who listened to the BBC and did nothing else, but even these were liable to be fined, imprisoned or deported as the repression intensified, while distributing or merely possessing a clandestine tract was a risk which could lead to torture and execution at the hands of the Gestapo. The history of the Resistance media is thus far more than a war of words; it involved the liberty and lives of people, many of whose names are still known only in their own immediate locality.

Where the first, tentative meetings of like-minded people did not lead to a publication and a movement, but to other forms of action, the early history of their resistance tends to be more obscure and even more localized. On the borders of the demarcation line and on the frontiers with Switzerland and Spain, a new profession of 'passeur' sprang up, requiring intimate knowledge of the terrain and a shrewd sense of local attitudes. 'Passing' someone across the line or across the frontier was often a reflex action of human solidarity but it could also be a calculation of gain in a tight economy. Stories are rife, and usually exaggerated, of 'passeurs' who took the money and left their 'clients' stranded in unknown country short of the border, but within a year or so most 'passeurs' had been integrated into one or more 'réseaux d'évasion', escape networks which quickly found their own effective means of dealing with false and unscrupulous competitors. The diffuse and individualized experience of these passeurs makes their history difficult to write, but their existence from the very start of the occupation and their growing importance in all resistance activity, established certain country areas as centres of resistance as early as the artisan cellars of the provincial towns. In many ways the risks in the country were greater, for strangers were conspicuous in rural areas, and the peasantry was sedulously cultivated by Vichy propaganda in the first two years, to an extent that made rural alternatives to subversion and 'attentisme' far more of an overt rebellion than comparable action in the towns. The relativity of situation, opportunity and choice is not always acknowledged when comparisons are made between town and country in the difficult days of early resistance.

The escape networks were slowly evolved alongside or within the 'réseaux de renseignements', the intelligence networks which eventually undermined the security of the German forces in France. The military importance of amateur intelligence work was far more slowly recognized by the British than the usefulness of a passeur who could secure the escape of a stranded pilot, and the problem was further complicated by the British policy of sending intelligence agents into France in preference to building on the initiatives made by French people already in the area. Espionage and intelligence have a code and professionalism all of their own, and the difficulties, for example, of an imaginative group of country gentry in the Dordogne, led by Louis de la Bardonnie, in convincing London that their information on German military installations and manoeuvres was valuable, should surprise nobody. What needs to be underlined is the persistence of de la Bardonnie's group, and many others, in collecting and dispatching information, so that eventually the agents sent by British intelligence, and by de Gaulle, were forced to integrate their activity with the untrained volunteers who knew the country and the language even if they were strangers to the code and the profession.

A movement distributing a newspaper, and a network engaged in escape or intelligence, appear to be quite different forms of resistance. But the movements were never limited to clandestine publishing, but from the start envisaged a plurality of action which included the gathering of intelligence, internal lines of transit, military preparations and innumerable services which would equip resisters with false papers and ration-books, look after the safety of their families, penetrate the Vichy administration and eventually establish rural hiding places and encampments for those who were on the run or who refused the compulsory labour service in Germany. When all these activities are given their rightful colour and texture in the mosaic of the Resistance, it can be seen that Resistance was an alternative way of life within occupied France, a society within a society, a power within and against the established powers of Vichy and the German authorities. As such it drew on the skills and knowledge of people as disparate as clerks in the town halls who made copies of legal documents, to mechanics in rural garages and farms who serviced the only lorry which could transport recruits, food and arms to the nearby woods. Being a resister was often living an ordinary life and working in a conventional job, but doing both in such a way as to favour the cause of Resistance and disadvantage the cause of Vichy and the Germans. A movement of Resistance was essentially a structure which initiated and coordinated these diffuse activities of everyday survival, and shaped them into a force to combat the occupation by every means possible, including armed attacks of a guerrilla kind. Only large-scale military confrontation was excluded. Apart from that, the Resistance was a society at war with Germany and its collaborators, but it was a war which Germany refused to recognize so that resisters were treated as terrorists, and the conventions of war disregarded. The Germans and Vichy labelled the resisters as political insurgents, and the Resistance claim to patriotism was denounced as a cover for foreign infiltration. It was a line of propaganda which was not without its effect on some of the French population, not least because there *were* strong political aspects to the Resistance and there *were* agents from Britain and eventually America whose access to money and arms gave them a degree of importance in Resistance organization way beyond their numerical strength.

The political aspects of Resistance break into two: politics *and* Resistance and the politics *of* Resistance. The first of these two is often obscured by the special pleading of political parties after the war when it was clearly important to establish good Resistance credentials before submitting to the electorate. But really it is not a particularly difficult subject to summarize for in no way can the first tentative moves towards Resistance be called the achievement of party politics. The Communist party had been stunned by the Nazi-Soviet pact in August 1939, had then been dissolved and made illegal by Daladier, and spent the next year and a half trying to resolve two sets of intractable contradictions. Firstly there was the party's excellent record of anti-fascism which seemed totally contradicted by Stalin's new policy, and secondly there was the long tradition of centralization in the party which was severely undermined by breaks in liaison with the outlying regions caused by the wave of arrests and imprisonments. The result was a restless and deeply unsatisfying period for the party, in which its leaders followed Stalin and officially condemned Germany, Britain and France in equal measure for the war and gave no instructions to its members to oppose the German occupiers, but one in which communists at the grass roots often continued their anti-fascism independently and began moves to combat the Germans as well as Vichy. Communist resistance before June 1941 included actions by the miners in May 1941 and the first steps towards sabotage launched by youth groups round Paris organized by Albert Ouzoulias, as well as other individual initiatives in Brittany, in Limoges and in the southern towns.

Such isolated actions kept the party's anti-fascist credentials from being totally negated by its subservience to Stalin's foreign policy, but no amount of reconstruction of the period September 1939 to June 1941 can equate the action of these communist individuals with official party policy. As individuals, many communists began to resist the Germans before Hitler invaded Russia in June 1941: as a *party* the communists did not. Nor did the Socialist party, the Radical party, or the Catholic Democratic party – all to the left of centre in the chamber elected to fight fascism in 1936, though once again there were individuals or splinter groups who partly salvaged the reputation of their parties, in particular the early actions of a group of socialists who formed a special Action Committee in the winter of 1940–1 across both zones. If there was any major difference between the Communist party and the other parties of the Popular Front in the first year of occupation it was this: the Communist party gave a clear lead in its rejection of Vichy and Pétain, but was of no help to its members in deciding what to do about the German occupiers, whereas the other parties were of no help to their member on *either* issue.

The Communist party survived its contradictions through the strength of its clandestine reorganization and the continuity of its press. Once the Nazi-Soviet pact was well and truly buried, the party was well placed to develop resistance organizations of its own and to harness its structures and media to the fight of all French people, and not just communists, against German occupation. From 1941 to the Liberation it was both a political and organizational pioneer in armed resistance, and its major movement, the Front National, was always a movement apart from the others, even though links on the ground made it an integral part of French Resistance as a whole. By contrast, no other party retained its structures during the occupation, and the Socialist Action Committee, as the only comparable voice on the Left, kept its political profile low, and did not try to refloat the Socialist party as a distinctive movement in the Resistance, though it did restart the party's main paper, *Le Populaire*.

No Resistance movement, therefore, apart from the Front National, was formally linked to a political party, although individual socialists were prominent in Libération (Nord) and Libération (Sud), while Catholic Democrats were more prominently involved in Combat, and there were Radicals at the start of Franc-Tireur. But just as there were non-communists in the Front National, there were communists in all the other movements. The way in which people first became involved in one or other movement was often linked to a tendency of pioneers to recruit among like-minded political friends, but as each movement grew beyond a small circle, it became more and more politically diffuse. The politics *of* Resistance took over.

The complications here were not really evident until 1942. Until then the various movements inside France, and de Gaulle's Free French movement outside, had their separate histories of growth and development. The Free French started as a military organization but rapidly developed a concern for propaganda, espionage, ideology, civil relations and politics which took it way beyond the competence of a few army and navy officers, while the internal movements started from a broader, civilian base and moved towards military action. Their paths met in 1942, but by then the different character of the movements and the understandable reluctance of leaders to relinquish their own visions and organizational achievements, made for two years of intense negotiations, necessary compromises and uneven commitment to the sharing of information and resources. It is not easy to see how it could have been different. The degree of complexity in producing a united Resistance should be seen as a positive sign of the plurality and diversity of resistance and not as a negative sign of fragmentation and pettiness.

Jean Moulin is the name rightly associated with both the difficulties and the success of the negotiations which brought the Free French and the French Resistance together. Sent by de Gaulle on several missions to France in early 1942, he rapidly discovered the tenacity with which different Resistance groups in France could hold to their own history, and the increasingly important role being played by the communists. Despite political hesitation in London he insisted that any successful coordination of the Resistance would have to involve the communists, however loosely, but that failing a complete integration the Resistance should at least unite the major non-communist movements into a single federated structure. His betrayal, torture and execution in the summer of 1943 occurred before his ambitious plan was fully realized, but during the 18 months of intensive, secret meetings, Jean Moulin became not only the epitome of the shadowy, romantic agent with his brown felt hat pulled over one eye, but also the symbol of rational planning and centralized provision.

Moulin did not make the best of relations with all the leaders inside France. Henri Frenay, the leader of Combat, saw him as mounting a takeover operation by the Gaullists, and as someone for whom the politics of a kind of clandestine Popular Front were more important than the tight organization of a secret army, and long after the war he accused Moulin of having made too many concessions to the communists. The controversy is fuelled every year by new sets of memoirs, but the reputation of Moulin is barely affected. Before his death the Mouvements Unis de la Résistance (MUR) was formed from Combat, Libération (Sud) and Franc-Tireur, and de Gaulle was acknowledged by these movements as a leader, even if only for some as a symbol. There was also a Co-ordinating Committee in the occupied zone, but the Front National remained separate from both, though working relations had been made and the communists were represented on the Conseil National de la Résistance (CNR) which was Moulin's final achievement within France and which proceeded to plan the political future of France in a bold, reforming charter.

In the summer of 1942, after advice from the socialist Christian Pineau, de Gaulle sent a message to the internal Resistance, in which he spoke not only of planning the Liberation, but also of preparing a revolution, and although that could be seen as an evocative phrase without much substance, his commitment to restore France to a republican form of democratic government was precise. The intrepid military pioneer of 18 June 1940 with past links to the right-wing Action Française now presented himself as a pillar of republican orthodoxy. Only by doing so was he able to gain the allegiance of the dominantly left-wing Resistance movements. His message was the clearest sign of the impact of representatives sent from the internal Resistance to London, and of de Gaulle's need for a political mandate to use in his constant arguments with Britain and America. This crucial development was not achieved by personality alone. Moulin, like Pierre Brossolette who had been an envoy before him, exercised sensitivity and persuasion, but he also dispensed money, and money in impoverished underground movements was power. How he dispensed it, and to whom, was naturally a controversial subject, no less than the money arriving in France through the British networks of SOE whose agents worked partly alongside and partly in competition with those sent by de Gaulle. Most of the money came ultimately from the same source – the British government – and so later did the most vital commodity, arms. Not surprisingly, therefore, the minor differences in Gaullist and SOE 'patronage' or supply are less important than the overall similarity of their practices. Money and arms went to those who accepted not only leadership but also a degree of strategic and tactical control. The communists had overtly rejected this in the autumn of 1941 when they authorized armed action against individual officers of the German army. De Gaulle condemned these acts as premature and provocative and claimed that he *alone* would decide when the time for armed attacks on the German army should take place. He pointed to the tragedy of hostages who were shot by the Germans in reprisal, but the communists argued that their actions put the Germans on the defensive and that for every French person arrested and shot by the occupiers, 50 joined the Resistance to avenge the innocent dead. There was no resolution to this tactical clash. Money and arms from London, and later from Algiers, did not flow into the Front National, nor into its armed and guerrilla section, the Francs-Tireurs et Partisans Français (FTPF). Instead it went to the networks, to the MUR, to its active wing the Armée Secrète and eventually to the *maquis* units which acknowledged the chain of allied and Gaullist command.

This unequal distribution of resources was the ultimate demonstration of just how important the politics of Resistance had become. Few resisters talked about arms in 1940. By 1943–4 arms and supplies had become the most vital ingredients in Resistance. They had to come from the Allies, just as the extreme collaborators looked for arms from the Germans. There ensued an armed struggle between Resistance and Collaboration within France, particularized by the embittered confrontation of Maquis and Milice, and in the last 18 months of the occupation this struggle took on increasingly the forms of civil war.

5 Liberation

In April 1942 Pierre Laval had returned to power in Vichy and had started a series of negotiated deals with the Germans. He made concessions in advance, and met the growing German demands with a mixture of collaboration and stubbornness which made sure that he remained the most hated of the Vichy ministers, but also caused some of the German leaders to complain that he was obstructing their grand design in Europe. It was with Fritz Sauckel, the Nazi Minister for Labour, that he had the most ambivalent relationship. Sauckel informed the French in the spring of 1942 that French labour was needed in Germany, and Laval proposed a scheme whereby volunteer workers would go from France and, in return, prisoners of war would be sent back from Germany. When finally the scheme (la Relève) was announced to the French in a speech on 22 June 1942, Laval prefaced it by words in which he declared his wish for 'the victory of Germany' as an insurance against 'the triumph of Bolshevism' in Europe. The first words of this statement 'Je souhaite la victoire de l'Allemagne', became the best-known words of the occupation, effacing even those of Marshal Pétain, and when Laval was shot after the Liberation it was as much for these words as anything. A major step in Vichy's downward path seemed to have been taken, though in essence Laval's response to Sauckel was not as submissive as Darlan's response to Hitler had been in circumstances more favourable to the French a year before.

The Relève gave way to a mixture of voluntary and press-ganged labour in the autumn of 1942, and finally to the compulsory registration and deportation of workers in the Service du Travail Obligatoire (STO) decreed by Laval in February 1943. The numbers Sauckel demanded were increased every few months, and Laval urged his prefects to meet the numbers in every way possible while minimizing the effect on French industries. At first he protected agricultural workers, students and women from registration, but this position was slowly eroded by the German insistence on ever-increasing targets and by Laval's own determination to survive with a semblance of negotiable power at his disposal. Sauckel protested to Hitler in a letter to the Führer of 9 August 1943 that Laval was dragging his feet; and Laval circulated his prefects with a justification of his policy on 2 March 1944, claiming that the figures showed that a smaller percentage of workers had been taken from France than from any of the neighbouring occupied countries. Historians admit the statistics, but point out that the Resistance was more responsible than Laval for the shortfall in the numbers, since from the spring of 1943 an increasing percentage of those called for service in Germany failed to appear and either went into hiding in isolated farms and villages, or joined Resistance units in the Maquis.

A close examination of the archives now reveals that Laval eventually adopted the same policy towards the requisition of labour as he did towards the deportation of Jews. In the summer of 1942 he did everything in his power to round up Jews with *foreign* origins, including those who had become naturalized in the 13 years before the war, and he ordered his administrators and police to collaborate tightly with the occupiers in piling these foreign Jews – men, women and children – into railway trucks and handing them over to the SS. Convoys numbering over 15,000 were sent in this way from the southern zone, still unoccupied, in August and September 1942. More were to follow when the Germans took over the area in November 1942. It was a policy of inhumanity given a specious nationalist morality by Laval's claim that he thereby protected the French Jews from the same fate. Similarly, as Sauckel's demands for labour escalated in 1943, Laval's circulars to the prefects show his determination to ransack the towns and countryside for marginalized workers, whose departure could be shown to have 'spared' the national workforce. But such workers could not be found in the numbers required, and eventually young workers and students were literally shunted from the Chantiers de la Jeunesse onto trains for Germany to make up the local contingents. Had he been able to satisfy Sauckel with the workers he deemed less worthy of protection he would have done so.

In this lies Laval's claim to have enacted the 'shield' philosophy of Vichy to the limits of his power. Certainly a case can be made, but it thrives on the categorization of some people as more expendable than others and it ignores what the effect on German resources might have been had the occupiers received no help at all in any of their deportation policies, in a country as large and difficult to administer as France. As it was, Sauckel's policy that labour should be brought into the Reich was being contested as inefficient by the technocrat Albert Speer. In the last six months of the occupation Speer was winning the argument and workers were being supervised in French industries in a cost-efficient preference to their removal to Germany. As for the deportation of Jews, the Vichy 'shield' must be compared with the much greater effectiveness of the Italians in the small corner of France which they occupied from November 1942 to the fall of Mussolini in July 1943. In those eight months, thousands of foreign Jews were protected by the Italian authorities in defiance of the Germans and the Vichy government, both of whom argued for their deportation. It seems a curiously humane epilogue to the violent history of Italian fascism, but a significant one nevertheless, for although Mussolini himself was far from consistent in his reaction to Nazi pressure, his army, police and administrators in France, Croatia and Greece, all contrived to protect the foreign Jews who came within their jurisdiction. The same can not be said of Vichy: in fact, quite the contrary. Laval expressed a personal determination that all immigrant and refugee Jews should be deported, particularly those whom the Germans themselves had expelled from the Palatinate and Alsace-Lorraine in 1940, and whom Vichy had crammed into concentration camps in the south-west of France, where many hundreds died of disease and malnutrition before the tragic journeys back to the East.

In the occupied zone the 'shield' philosophy was even more inoperative. There the Germans had initiated the first massive round-up of Jews on 16 July 1942. They were helped by 9,000 French police and administrators, and Vichy made no attempt to intervene when over 4,000 Jewish children were packed into a sports stadium, the Vélodrome d'Hiver, for five days without sanitation, water or adequate food, mostly separated from their parents who had been sent to other camps near Paris. The terror and suffering of these children had no effect on Laval. 'They must all go', he said when, for the first time, religious leaders of both the Catholic and Protestant churches protested against the effects of Vichy's collaboration.

The children from the Vélodrome d'Hiver were deported along with a total of over 70,000 other Jewish victims of Nazi and Vichy persecution. Most left from the transit camp at Drancy at which French police were on guard duty throughout the whole of the occupation, and which was actually administered by the French until July 1943, though it is certain that news of the mass exterminations of Auschwitz reached France by the autumn of 1942, if not before.

At this crucial turning point in Vichy's history, Marshal Pétain fell amost totally into the background, though his mystique was cultivated by the Vichy media as assiduously as ever. His occasional speeches on the radio confined themselves to declarations of support for Laval, and appeals for solidarity, law and order, patience and understanding, but his relative inaction cannot be seen as a sign of disagreement with the overall trend of Vichy policy. Recent research has pointed to his share of moral responsibility for the deportation of the Jews and it is clear that his version of the shield philosophy was no less illusory than Laval's.

The German invasion of the southern zone on 11 November 1942 destroyed Pétain's claim to have saved a huge part of France from German occupation, while the Allied invasion, of North Africa severed the links between Vichy and the French Empire. Pétain ordered the French troops and authorities in North Africa to resist the Allies but Admiral Darlan, who had taken charge in Algeria, agreed to a ceasefire with the Allies and took both Algeria and French West Africa into a series of complicated negotiations with the Americans, trying to refloat his Vichy authority under American protection. Both Pétain and Laval rejected this tentative crossing into a form of 'collaboration' with the Allies, since their bargaining position with the Germans would have been totally destroyed had they supported Darlan. In fact the Germans were less interested than ever in Laval's frantic attempts to keep a line open between Vichy and Berlin, and Laval's visit to Hitler in early November failed to stop the German decision to occupy the whole of France, and failed to prevent the Germans from demanding the dissolution of the armistice army, on which Vichy's slender claims to some form of military independence had rested. Pétain submitted to this humiliation and, unwilling to command the navy to join the Allies in North Africa, submitted also to the scuttling of the Vichy fleet in Toulon, the only assertive action left to the navy commanders who felt unable to sail against Pétain's wishes but could not allow their ships to fall into German hands. Within a month, therefore, Vichy had lost its own zone of independence, its army, its fleet and its empire, and yet still Pétain felt it was his duty to remain as head of state, though many of his closest sympathisers, including Jean Borotra, urged him to leave France for his own safety. When Pétain refused, Borotra saw this as one more sacrifice by the 'saviour of France' who had once again 'put the interests of the country before his own' (interview with the author, April 1980). Others saw it as the opposite, the obstinate egoism of a man who still believed he was always right, or even more darkly as an ideological commitment to the Axis powers.

The messianic tone of the National Revolution was replaced by a defensive justification of Vichy as the only source of French authority in a world said to be increasingly threatened by either communism or chaos, and at a local level the public manifestations of Vichy, either through the Légion or through the youth movement, Compagnons de France, no longer had any substantial popular support, nor even interest. The prefects in their monthly reports to the Minister of the Interior admitted that public opinion was at best indifferent and, at worst, hostile and subversive, and they called for a reassertion of positive principles to win back the sympathy that had been there in 1940–1.

Reassertion they were given, but not in the way that most of them wanted. Instead of revitalized Pétainism with the myths refurbished, they had to decide whether to come to terms with their own declining authority or to lurch intemperately into a more overtly fascist-style regime. Most accepted the decline and even made a virtue of it, putting out feelers to local Resistance movements, turning a blind eye to failures of their own administration, or still further conniving at long bureaucratic delays in police activity which allowed those escaping from STO to remain untraced or become untraceable. But some made the assertive move into fascism and became patrons of the Milice, vigorously pursuing the hunt for *réfractaires* from STO, for communists thought to be behind every local disturbance, and for Resistance groups whom they accused of knowingly or unwittingly preparing the ground for a communist takeover.

It was not just the prefects who had to decide which way to go: at all levels of the Vichy state the decision presented itself, and at the top Laval gave most encouragement to those moving in the fascist direction. On the one hand he appeared to be holding the Paris fascists at bay, by his intense dislike of Doriot, the most flamboyant, populist candidate for Nazi patronage, and in his instructions to the administration he told them to preserve their independence from the German authorities. But on the other hand he brought Marcel Déat into the government in March 1944 as Minister of Labour, and had earlier promoted the head of the Milice, Joseph Darnand, to be the government official in charge of law and order. The latter appointment institutionalized the Milice as an arm of the state, alongside the mobile reserve units of the national police, the GMR, which joined the Milice as an auxiliary to the German SS and Gestapo. To most people who knew nothing of the nuances of his instructions to the civil service, this partnership with Darnand was the final proof that Laval was a committed fascist, and the workings of the special courts which he approved to bring resisters to trial further intensified this image. Laval's claim to 'double-jeu', giving a little to the occupiers to prevent them taking more, may ultimately have a balance sheet of losses and gains which will keep the argument alive, but his determination to enforce law and order through the Milice and the GMR, his policy that Vichy should be seen to be conscientious in its hunt for all internal dissidents, and finally his instructions to the local prefects to 'respect the terms of the Armistice' and maintain law and order as the Germans retreated, show that he made no effort to trim his policy to the winds of Resistance. It may be argued that in that respect at least he showed some integrity, but it means that he must be seen as less of an opportunist than he claimed, and more as an ideologue carried by his fear of communism into violent repression, racial antisemitism and a tacit acceptance of the methods practised by the Milice.

Created by Joseph Darnand in January 1943 from his position as head of the Légion in Nice, the Milice saw itself initially as the paramilitary vanguard of the National Revolution, intensely loyal to the person of Marshal Pétain, but in this it was already two years away from the high point of Pétainism, and its rationale in 1943–4 increasingly became the service of Vichy-style fascism and inexorably the service of the German authorities. Public opinion was totally opposed; and in the Lot the prefect summarized the opinions of himself and his *département* when he said in October 1943 (Laborie 1980, p. 272); 'The Milice are seen to be entirely in the pay of the Germans, and the least I can say is that it appears that this is so'. Their readiness to work with the Germans, explicitly and proudly admitted by Darnand in November 1943, gave them a power out of all proportion to their numbers, which remained in the lower hundreds in most *départements*, a mere fraction of the population who were sympathetic to Vichy. In no sense could the Vichy administration and the Milice be seen as coterminous, and most of the prefects refused to patronize their local unit. The Milice received arms from the Germans after an initial hesitation on the part of the occupiers, and this gave them the authority they needed to expose not just the activities of Resistance but also the shortcomings of the local police and their authorities. Composed for the most part of young men who had become rootless during the occupation and who used the Milice for quick promotion over their fellows, the Milice had the effect of edging some cautious Vichy personnel into nervous gestures of support, but more often finalized the rupture of the bourgeois administration from the brasher elements of collaborationism.

The Milice was authorized to spread into the occupied zone in January 1944 and by March had joined the German army in military action against the Resistance in the Alpine foothills of the Glières. Its speciality was the capture and torture of resisters who became cut off in remote villages, and the murder of known Republican person-alities, notably Jean Zay, the pre-war Minister of Education, and Georges Mandel, Clemenceau's close friend and colleague. In Paris the Miliciens rivalled the militants of Doriot's PPF as infiltrators in the Resistance networks, and Darnand himself joined Doriot in the uniform of the Nazis. With Philippe Henriot's verbal attacks on the Maquis, broadcast throughout provincial France, and the combined operation of the Milice and the GMR, collaborationist France launched a final assault on the growing tide of Resistance in the early summer of 1944. The Milice were fighting a civil war which Vichy insisted had never begun.

For the Resistance 1942–3 was also the major turning-point. Outside France the unfolding history of de Gaulle's Free French, now known as La France Combattante, developed into a decisive struggle for recognition by the Allies. When the Americans and British decided on the landing in North Africa in November 1942, de Gaulle was not consulted despite the fact that Churchill had accepted the National Committee of the Free French as the authentic representative of all French people who were determined to continue the war. Still worse from de Gaulle's point of view, the Americans insisted on negotiating with the Vichy administration in Algeria and offering the leadership of the French forces to Admiral Darlan. This identified the central task of the Gaullists only too clearly. Either they had to stamp themselves beyond any doubt as the voice of France, or they would be ignored by the Americans with the result that France would be treated as a vassal country at the Liberation and would have little say in its own post-war future and no voice at all in the future of Europe. The result was the acceleration of de Gaulle's negotiations with the Resistance movements and his open willingness to discuss any political matters with representatives of the old political parties, several of whom were crossing to London to impress on de Gaulle the extent of Resistance hostility to the internal politics of Vichy. The communists joined this political lobbying, sending Fernand Grenier in January 1943, while the socialist leader, Léon Blum, was also in contact with de Gaulle from the prison in which he was kept after he had skilfully turned the tables on Pétain at the fiasco of a trial which Vichy had staged at Riom in February 1942. To all these proponents of political republicanism, de Gaulle responded with enough assurances to minimize their suspicions, or in many cases to gain their enthusiastic support.

On 24 December 1942 Darlan was assassinated, but de Gaulle continued to need Resistance support in the second phase of his battle with the Americans, this time to outmanoeuvre Darlan's successor, General Giraud, who was a Pétainist but was unmarked by any hint of collaboration. He had even the image of a resister, having made a much-publicized escape from a German prisoner-of-war camp, and in all respects was a much more viable candidate for Eisenhower and Roosevelt to promote in their campaign against de Gaulle, whom they accused of dictatorial ambition and an unhealthy obsession with espionage and plots.

Churchill, however, remained the patron of de Gaulle, in whose cause the British government had invested millions of pounds, but the partnership came close to breaking in the first five months of 1943. There is a good deal of speculation that British intelligence had been behind the removal of the embarrassing figure of Darlan, but in this new phase of de Gaulle's fight for leadership in North Africa, the British government put pressure on him to compromise with Giraud and accept a joint leadership. Eventually de Gaulle agreed, but not before exceeding his considerable reputation in the eyes of the Allies for obstinacy and self-projection. Again, as in 1940, he held to his image of himself as the agent of French destiny, and his rival Giraud was given little credit for the important role he played in directing the army of French North Africa into the path of active cooperation with the Allies. But in no way was Giraud equally equipped for a conflict of power. He had none of the support which de Gaulle and the Free French had won within France and none of de Gaulle's political acumen. Once de Gaulle had arried in Algiers in the summer of 1943 he rapidly assumed control. By the end of the year the French Committee of National Liberation in Algiers was not only Gaullist in loyalty but was well on the way to becoming the provisional government of France with de Gaulle as undisputed leader.

Inside France in 1943 the Resistance moved into a military role without losing any of the rich complexity of its embryonic period. In response to the changed direction of the war and the growing harshness of the occupation, the Resistance movements all subordinated survival and protest to the preparation of a national insurrection. The circulation of newspapers and pamphlets, the collecting of information, the recruiting of new resisters in towns and villages previously untouched by the rigours of the occupation but now submitted to the regular patrol of German troops, all these activities continued and expanded, but the vital new ingredient was provided by the pressures of Sauckel and the collaboration of Laval. From the moment that labour service became compulsory the logistics of Resistance took on an urgency which demanded new resources, new strategies, and an entirely new cover, the woods.

forests and hills of rural France, called after the Corsican word for scrubland, the *maquis*, a word by which the armed Resistance bands soon became known.

For a long time after the war historians assumed that there was an automatic passage of workers escaping from the STO into the Maquis. A more careful sifting of the evidence shows that this was neither as automatic nor as general as was once thought. It is true that from April to December 1943 about 150,000 men were at some point on the run from the STO, and from January to June 1944 more than double that number, and it is true that the Maquis bands, whether a handful of 20, or a company of several hundred, contained a significant percentage of these *réfractaires*. But in the early summer of 1943 there were few if any Maquis groups to which workers could immediately attach themselves. They had to be created, like the first groups of resisters, in 1940, and for many *réfractaires* this meant months of *ad hoc* arrangements, hiding in farms, taking on forestry work in return for food and shelter, or simply moving from village to village in search of either security or work. Many thousands drifted back to their homes and regularized their situation with the police, particularly once Vichy had made the attractive promise that those who gave themselves up would not be sent to Germany but would be employed in France. The majority who did not return home had to decide at some point whether to commit themselves to an armed and outlawed existence in the Maquis, or to survive as best they could in casual employment in the countryside, but in either case they increased the scope of Resistance activity.

Every Resistance movement, through its papers and pamphlets, called on workers to resist the STO and not to answer the final summons to report for what they called the 'deportation of slave labour'. To make this policy a realistic one, they had to expand their service of false papers and ration cards, to search out and guarantee safe places of hiding, and finally to provide the most committed *réfractaires* with leadership, arms, a strategy for action, and the food and clothes necessary for surviving a winter in the cruellest temperatures of the snow-covered hills and forests. Even those who did not become armed *maquisards*, but were nevertheless undermining the German war economy simply by being *réfractaires*, could legitimately call on the protection of the Resistance, and the Resistance movements had to extend well beyond their limited urban resources. Money, arms and supplies were eagerly sought from British and Gaullist parachute drops, and one of the first aims of most Maquis groups was to find a suitable clearing onto which the parachutes could be dropped at dead of night.

Only one thing was invariably more important, and that was to make sure that the local peasantry was sympathetic to the presence of the *maquisards*. The failure of Vichy to control the requisition of agricultural produce by an increasingly predatory German army, and the huge discrepancy between Vichy propaganda towards the peasants and hard economic results, made the task of the Resistance easier with every month that passed, and in 1944 many Maquis were created by the rural population themselves, once Laval lifted the exceptions which had protected the agricultural sector from the STO. Even so, hard and bitter relations between *maquisards* and the peasantry were not unknown, and gradually the Maquis learnt to protect peasant goods from requisition and to distribute the food, ration cards, tobacco and money, which they took from Vichy supply depots, among the local population as well as among their own units. In the Monts d'Auxois near Dijon imaginative Maquis leaders even devised a system of taxation on a sliding scale by which local collaborators were heavily 'taxed' at one end and sympathetic peasants received a 'tax bonus' at the other. In the Limousin countryside round Limoges, the Maquis leader Colonel Guingouin called himself the Prefect of the Maquis, so sure had he become of his power-base among the local peasantry; and in the thickly wooded hills of the Cévennes at the south of the Massif Central where the Protestant Camisards had fought against the central government in the early eighteenth century, their descendants re-used the old sheep tracks and took refuge in the hidden caves which had served the Camisards so well over 200 years before. In such ways the Maquis became a rural force dissolving the urban administrative control of Vichy, undermining its law and order, and leading certain areas into a revolt which was the most unexpected twist of events for a regime which had placed the eternal values of rural France at the head of its National Revolution.

But were the Maquis an effective armed force against the Germans, or even against the Milice? The question will be debated as long as historians write about the Resistance, for it contains so many other questions within it, and not a few of them are tendentiously posed for political reasons. It soon became apparent to the communists of the Front National that if their Maquis groups, the Francs-Tireurs et Partisans français (FTPF), were to have any arms or ammunition they would have to find it themselves. Neither the British nor the Gaullists were inclined to arm what they mistakenly believed were potential soviets in the countryside. The BBC even censored the word 'partisan' from a broadcast about France by the communist Fernand Grenier, even though the word was openly used about the guerrilla fighters in Yugoslavia. In fact the FTPF were locally known less for their political ideology than for their energy and activism, and several Maquis leaders like Jean Jacques Chapou from the region north of Toulouse left the Maquis bands of the Mouvements Unis de la Résistance, known as the Armée Secrète (AS), to join the more purposeful ranks of the FTPF. And yet in other areas the AS were better organized and the FTPF no more than small marauding bands with no strategic cohesion, while some Maquis were so autonomous that they belonged to neither major grouping and resented being typecast as either communist or Gaullist. But wherever there was a clear chain of command linking the *maquisards* to London or Algiers, as in the Montagne Noire in the Tarn, where the English agent known as Major Richardson was one of the local leaders, the certainty of receiving regular arms was infinitely higher than for the FTPF.

Within this imbalance of arms and ammunition, there was also a disagreement on basic strategy. The AS accepted the overall Gaullist and Allied strategy that the Maquis should hold themselves in readiness for an Allied landing, and then provide an internal support for the liberating Allied armies. For the FTPF this was too cautious and too submissive a role, and they argued that constant harrass-ment, sabotage and ambushes would tie down large numbers of Germans in the French countryside and prevent them from reinforcing the Eastern front, or from joining the Western front when it occurred. Cutting across this division of opinion and uniting most Maquis and urban resistance groups was the internal certainty that resisters could more effectively neutralize any railway depot, large industry or power station, than the British or American air force. Many British agents, notably Harry Rée of SOE, argued the same point with equal force, and Rée personally was responsible for extensive sabotage of the Peugeot works at Montbéliard with an efficiency of which a bombing raid was incapable. As for the sabotage of railways by the French railway workers, or by *maquisards* attacking exposed areas of line with primitive but effective explosive devices, the total effect on the movement of German goods and troops was massive, and would have been even more impressive had sufficient arms been dropped to regions like the Lozère, which the British throughout 1943 appeared unable to find on the map.

Measuring effectiveness is therefore a highly relative operation. It is certain that without the Allied supply of arms and the courageous activity of British and Gaullist pilots, agents and wireless operators, the Maquis would never have been an operational military force at all. But it can be argued with equal certainty that had the Maquis, of

71

all kinds, been more trusted and more intensively armed and supplied, then more French men and women could have been withdrawn from German industries within France, and far more *réfractaires* kept in active Maquis units. The result in terms of increased German material losses might have been substantial.

What size the Maquis units should have been has also been the subject of extended controversy. At the time there were leaders who were convinced that small mobile units of 20–30 men, able to leave a hiding place overnight and move to another, were the model size, but there were others who believed the Maquis could only play an important part in Allied strategy if they were grouped in considerable numbers, able to hold down a sizeable unit of the German army. In pursuit of the latter idea a plan was formed by a group including Jean Moulin and General Delestraint, the head of the AS, to group several hundreds of Resistance fighters in the Alpine mountains of Haute Savoie and the Isère, and to give them a major military role at the time of the Allied invasions. The result was two major tragedies in March and July 1944, when first the Germans and the French Milice destroyed a Maquis unit of over 450 men in the Glières, and then the Wehrmacht and SS killed over 800 *maquisards* and villagers, many in cold blood, on the plateau of the Vercors. Was it the fault of the plan? It appears that it never reached the Allied High command. Did the Maquis in the Glières assemble too early? It seems that they did, but their survival might have been possible had they been better armed, even though the British dropped 90 tons of arms in one night in early March. Were the Vercors Maquis left to their fate by an inflexible Allied command and did they fail to receive the massive help promised by Gaullist leaders in Algiers? The bulk of the evidence suggests that the Vercors was indeed the victim of both Allied and Gaullist decisions not to send last-minute reinforcements, despite the most moving telegrams from the beleaguered Resistance fighters.

In between these two Alpine tragedies, the area of Mont Mouchet in the Auvergne saw over 5,000 *maquisards* respond to what was essentially a 'levée en masse', at the end of May 1944. The Germans attacked in force on 10 June and met a surprising resistance from the poorly armed French fighters, but the Maquis leaders saw the wisdom and the possibility of dispersing before a second attack, and the retreat was ordered during the night. The vast majority of the Maquis escaped to other parts of the Massif Central, and although the losses of the *maquisards* were heavy, so too were those of the German forces in the first assault. Not all large groupings of the Maquis were thus condemned to tragedy, but the huge scale of the Mont Mouchet operation was not repeated in the area, even when the Germans began to retreat after the Allied landings in Provence. The Maquis of the Massif Central regrouped in much smaller units, and the lasting impression of Maquis history given by most *maquisards* in oral interviews is that the limited supply of arms and the uncertainty of Allied strategy towards the Resistance made such smaller, mobile operations the only viable tactics for the Maquis. But the arguments will long continue, not least because if courage against overwhelming odds is a valid criterion in assessing the Maquis, then many a mobile group which survived intact in the woods will honour those who were killed in pitched encounters on a mountainous plateau from which escape had become impossible.

The dramas of the rural Maquis should not efface the resistance of the towns, where the conflict with the Milice and the Gestapo was an everyday event, and torture or deportation an everyday reality. From the spring of 1944 the Germans decided the local Vichy administration could not be trusted to enforce the STO, to pursue resisters, or to round up the Jews whose mass elimination was being ever more hysterically demanded by Hitler and Himmler as the war turned decisively against them. With local variations in severity, they proceeded to round up any individuals they felt might be *réfractaires*, resisters or Jews and deport them without appeal. When the Vichy administration protested or tried to intervene, the Germans threatened to deport the mayors and the prefects, and in many cases between June and August 1944 did so. Not surprisingly the resignation rate of Vichy personnel in this period reached epidemic proportions, and Vichy as a state collapsed at local level well before its political leaders followed the Germans into retreat. The local police (gendarmerie) had been thoroughly infiltrated by the Resistance in 1943 or even earlier, as had the Post Office and the railways. All that was left in 1944 for the Germans to depend on was the Milice, the mobile units of the national police, and a handful of ideologically sympathetic prefects and junior administrators. With the mass of the country passively supporting the Resistance if not actively engaged, the determination of these remaining collaborators to damage the Resistance as much as possible before the Liberation occurred, not surprisingly provoked a level of hatred which only civil wars appear able to produce.

It was not a civil war, in the sense of Spain in 1936–9 or Russia after the Revolution, since collaboration in the Laval mould had never won over a substantial part of the population, and the collaborationism and fascism into which it degenerated could claim only a few thousand supporters at most. But where the Milice were involved there was a ferocity of feeling which made people talk of treason, with a summary execution always in mind, and most Miliciens were shot either before the Liberation or just after without any second thoughts either by the Resistance or the rest of the population, and there is little evidence that the new archive information available will provide a base for their rehabilitation in the eyes of history.

Alongside this hatred of the extreme collaborators there grew an impatient anxiety about the long-expected Allied landing on the shores of France, whenever and wherever it was to be. Jour-J, as D-Day was called in France, was first thought to be imminent in the autumn of 1943, but autumn, winter and the spring of 1944 all passed without the opening of the offensive for which so much Resistance activity was primed. Finally, when the non-existent event was becoming something of a bitter joke, particularly among communist resisters who had kept the country informed of the courage and losses of the Russian army on the Eastern front, the crucial day was announced on the BBC in a sequence of coded messages on the night of 5–6 June 1944. The anxieties were forgotten: the Liberation of France had begun.

The brilliant planning of D-Day, code-named Overlord, and the secrecy of the vast operation, were the Allied equivalent of Guderian's crossing of the Meuse in 1940. It was not that the German armies in France were defeated as fast as the British and French had been, but that Hitler and his generals produced the same kind of failures of command in the face of the invasion. No tactical withdrawal and regrouping was permitted by the Führer, so that the Germans were spread thinly across the north of France, allowing the vital penetrations to be made by the Americans from the Cotentin peninsular through to Avranches, and the British from a month of heavy fighting at Caen through to Falaise. These breakthroughs secured the D-Day objectives by the end of July, and the Allied forces began a rapid sweep through Normandy into north-east France and Belgium where they arrived in early September. The route of German victory in June 1940 was now the route of German retreat, and the civilian *exode* and panic of 1940 was now the tumultuous civilian acclaim and welcome which greeted the British, American, Canadian and French troops in the liberated villages and towns.

This welcome was not without its ambivalence, since destruction in Normandy caused by the intensive Allied bombing before and during the D-Day operations left a permanent scar in the collective memory of the region, and raised dramatically the question of

74

whether a properly armed Resistance could have destroyed many of the military targets with a mere fraction of the civilian losses. The BBC messages had been enthusiastically received by the Resistance throughout France and the various plans for mobilization were put into effect. The Armée Secrète (AS) and the Francs-Tireurs et Partisans Français (FTPF) had been brought into one organization called the Forces Françaises de l'Intérieur (FFI), but the state of armament in most Resistance groupings was lamentable. Nevertheless the French commander of the FFI, General Koenig, who had led a French army to the famous victory over Rommel at Bir Hakeim in Libya in June 1942, estimated that 60 percent of the Jour-J plans for the Resistance were effectively carried out, including the paralysis of railways in the regions closest to the Normandy beaches, the destruction of high-tension electric cables in the same areas, and the harrassment of German troops making their way from the south into the battle zone.

The German archives amply document the success of the Resistance in delaying and diverting the German troops which were heading northwards, and at the end of June General Eisenhower stated that the help of the Resistance in the D-Day operations had been worth a full 15 divisions. It was an achievement shared jointly by the French resisters themselves and the various SOE agents, Jedburgh missions and troops of the Special Air Service, who had been sent with money, arms and military skills into the Resistance, but despite this record of achievement behind the German lines many military accounts of the Normandy landings and the Liberation of northern France are still written with no reference to the role of Resistance. Nor is the presence of French troops always acknowledged, even though the Second French Division of General Leclerc was given a place in the landings and was permitted to make a detour to Paris in order to secure the surrender of the German garrison there after the Parisian Resistance had launched its own assault on the Germans, had taken over the Prefecture of Police and had erected barricades in many parts of the city.

As the Allied armies pushed on to the north of Paris into Belgium, the FFI were left with the task of liberating Brittany, which they achieved by October with the exception of the ports of Lorient and Saint-Nazaire where the Germans had enough heavy armament to hold out against the light weapons of the Resistance until the end of the war. Elsewhere in France, in the centre and south, the German retreat was accelerated by the second Allied landing, in Provence on 15 August, and by the national insurrection of the Maquis who effectively finalized the liberation of most of France west of the

Rhône and south of the Loire. In the landings in Provence, the First French Army under General de Lattre de Tassigny was given the role of liberating the Rhône valley and Lyon while the Americans pressed eastwards through Grenoble, and the success of the landings, code-named Anvil, was such that a meeting of the liberating troops from north and south was affected at Montbard in Burgundy on 11–12 September, less than a month after the first fighting on the coastline near St Tropez.

It was during the German retreat that the war, from which so much of France had escaped in 1940, finally came to most parts of the country. Some leaders of the Wehrmacht were prepared to negotiate a withdrawal with the local Resistance, and in Paris the military governor, General von Choltitz, refused to destroy the city as Hitler commanded. But in most instances the German army, subject to ambush at every turn in the road, retaliated by shooting prisoners and destroying farms and even villages. The worst atrocities were committed by the SS Division Das Reich which left a trail of destruction from the south-west of France in early June, culminating in the execution of 99 hostages at Tulle in the Corrèze and the shooting and burning of over 600 men, women and children in the village of Oradour-sur-Glâne, south of Limoges. It is here, and in many other remote places in rural France, that monuments to *maquisards* and hostages tell some of the history of Hitler's war which official accounts of the major battles often relegate to the foot-notes.

In summary, what did the Liberation of France involve for those who had created the history of collaboration and resistance since 1940? For Vichy leaders, it was the moment when their subservience to Germany was fully exposed. In July 1944 both Pétain and Laval tried to contact de Gaulle to propose a shared provisional govern-ment, and when they received no reply, Laval attempted to persuade Edouard Herriot, the leader of the old Radical party and President of the Chamber of Deputies under the Third Republic, to call a National Assembly. To Abetz he declared his determination to find a French solution to the end of Vichy which would be honourable to all sides, but he was whistling in the dark. On 18 August Berlin confirmed previous orders to Abetz that the Vichy government should be taken to Belfort under German 'protection'. Pétain refused to leave, but had no choice. The Vichy regime was taken hostage by Germany and installed in a small town on the Danube in Baden-Würtemburg. There, at Sigmaringen, in a castle which had belonged to the Hohenzollerns, the collaborators from Vichy and the collaborationists from Paris were thrown together for the first time. To his deep humiliation Marshal Pétain ended his political career under the same roof as Jacques Doriot.

For the internal Resistance, the Liberation was the triumphal justification of Republican patriotism, of anti-fascism and a faith in the fight for freedom which had seemed 'absurd' in 1940, but which by August 1944 had become so accepted that post-war France looked back on Resistance activity as the 'normal' behaviour of all French people. This it had never been. It was the painful creation of a minority, for which the majority eventually showed enthusiasm, but few urban resisters, and even fewer *maquisards*, had any illusions about the eleventh-hour recruits who flooded the FFI in July and August. For this reason there was a fortnight after the Liberation in August 1944 when old scores were settled, and summary judgements were carried out by Resistance tribunals to purge each locality of its collaborators. No Resistance historian should try to minimize the incidents of injustice, malicious indictment and personal vendetta which stained the record of some Resistance units, but no-one reading the minutes of the local liberation committees can fail to see the emotive importance of the purges. In the months following the Liberation hardly a day passed without some new revelation of the horrors of torture, deportation and execution for which Gestapo and Milice had been responsible, and as the shallow graves of mutilated resisters were found in country areas surrounding most of the large towns, and the cellars of the Gestapo revealed their inhuman secrets, the popular demand for retributive justice against the collaborators grew more insistent. But in contrast to a mythology which grew up later that over a 100,000 people were executed at the Liberation, the real figures have been authoritatively calculated from official records as between 10,000 and 12,000, and as courts replaced the Resistance tribunals the number of acquittals soon exceeded the number of convictions.

More generally the picture emerges of a period of euphoria when Resisters bridged the local vacuum of power with an assertive display of popular, patriotic ideals, setting up local committees to administer supplies, to organize recruitment for the army, and to relaunch their communities on a more equal, just and fraternal footing. There have been few occasions in French history since 1789 when the slogans of the Revolution have commanded such universal respect. For a month at least, before the weight of restructuring the economy and continuing the war began to sap people's optimism, there was a widespread belief that French society could be recast to give equal opportunities to everyone. It was an ideal to which resisters look back with pride. It was a period, say many, when very

77

ordinary men and women were momentarily in charge of their own history.

This period of popular power in certain parts of France was short-lived. Most of the liberation committees had been picked well in advance by Resistance groups in which loyalty to de Gaulle was significant, if not paramount. From Algiers the structures of administrative power had been carefully planned to make sure that the Americans could find no reason for imposing a military occupation. Safe appointments were made to ensure a solid transfer of power, and in almost all cases these structures held, even when temporarily shaken by local Maquis assertiveness. The communists were equally concerned to show responsibility, for the war was not yet over and there could not be elections until the fighting was finally stopped. Fears, or hopes, of a communist revolution, were equally groundless. De Gaulle received criticism but no opposition from his communist colleagues in the provisional government. They posed no serious threat to his assumption of power, and at local level they were often a restraining force on those who saw a chance for a major social and political change.

For the external Resistance the Liberation was the moment when de Gaulle, the symbol of protest and resistance, became the embodiment of power. His personal triumph was extraordinary, and when he walked the length of the Champs-Elysées on 26 August, the day after Paris had been finally liberated by the internal Resistance and the French division of General Leclerc, the acclamations of the crowd sealed the epic position which he had won in the history of France. Paris was once again the capital of France, a position which had been usurped by Vichy on the one hand, and by the towns of Marseille, Montpellier, Toulouse, Grenoble, Limoges, and above all, Lyon, on the other, where the Resistance movements had established their centres of operation. De Gaulle acknowledged this at once by announcing a tour of the provinces, and in September he was wildly acclaimed in Lyon, and also in Marseille, though it was there that his unwillingness to unbend and talk informally to the local Maquis leaders was first publicly noted. In Toulouse he was even more insistent on his dignity, and only just managed to rescue a meeting with *maquisards* from disaster, but he then excluded Limoges altogether from his tour, sending a deputy instead with directions to assert the provisional government's authority over the local Resist-ance. This became comparatively easy to achieve once the Maquis in all parts of France had been absorbed into the army – a move which was necessary but which was insensitively proposed in the first place, and left many Maquis units convinced that their hopes of a new kind of egalitarian army had been deliberately betrayed from the top. Insensitive and arrogant he certainly was, but it was these qualities which had characterized de Gaulle's entire Resistance history, and the results could be argued to have told in his favour. France was *not* treated by the Allies as a country deserving reprimand for its collaboration: it was treated as a co-belligerent and an independent ally. De Gaulle was not the French Resistance: he never had been, but the Resistance was prepared to acknowledge his power in 1944 and to express its gratitude for his leadership. It would have been the mark of a really great leader had he done more to understand what had happened at the grass roots. At that level the Resistance had been a matter not just of leadership but of equality and comradeship. De Gaulle could not accept the revolutionary potential of that experience.

The Vichy regime disappeared with the Liberation, but its leaders were brought back from Germany for trial, after the Allies, now joined by France, had defeated the Nazi Reich. Doriot had been killed inside Germany in an attack by an unidentified aircraft, and Déat escaped to a convent in Turin where he was hidden until his death. Darquier de Pellepoix, the venemous anti-semite, escaped to Spain, and several local leaders of the Milice also disappeared into self-imposed exile. Laval, Darnand, and de Brinon were all tried, found guilty of treason and executed: so too were the novelist and journalist Robert Brasillach, the newspaper owner Jean Luchaire, and the broadcaster Jean-Hérold Paquis. Marshal Pétain and the ideologue of Action Française, Charles Maurras, were also condemned to death, but spared execution due to their old age. Both died in supervised residence, Pétain outside the shores of France on the Ile d'Yeu. Both had been subjected to national degradation which included their removal from the Académie Française.

As the trials were staged, France was playing a full role in the final months of the war, or coming to terms with a peace which revealed the first appalling statistics of those who had died in the concentration camps or had returned in varying states of physical and mental debility. It was not easy to mitigate justice with calls for compassion or statements of Vichy's ambiguity, and the trials in France have raised the same kind of moral and judicial doubts as those held in Nuremburg. Laval's claim to have played a double-game (*double-jeu*) in order to shield the French was not considered as a case that should be presented, and with Pétain refusing to acknowledge the legality of his trial, neither of the two main Vichy leaders was able to argue the Vichy case. Historians since have frequently 'restaged' the trials, as more and more evidence becomes available, and such reconsiderations will continue long into the next century when the last Vichy documents are scheduled to be released. Nothing has so far emerged which substantially alters the grounds for the verdicts of 1945, and the pressure of a small group of Pétainist devotees who want the Marshal rehabilitated continues to meet the reasonable objection that his authority was the cloak under which Vichy collaboration and fascism had so much freedom to develop.

The events of 1942–4 put Pétain back into the fallible world of politics from which the process of mythification had elevated him. Historians with a weakness for cyclical theories of history like to suggest that the vacuum created was filled with a new myth, the myth of the Resistance, and a new mythic figure, that of General de Gaulle. It is a tempting conclusion but a false one. Both Resistance history and Gaullism have been given an epic treatment which suggests a kind of myth-making, but no one who has seriously investigated the Resistance to Nazism, whether in France or elsewhere, finds it either easy or necessary to question its exceptional achievements. The history of Resistance may read excitingly as fiction. It reads even more effectively as fact.

Guide to Further Reading

Amouroux, H. 1976 –:*La Grande Histoire des Français sous l'Occupation*. 7 vols. Laffont.

Amouroux, H. 1961: *La Vie des Français sous l'Occupation*. 2 vols. Fayard.

Azéma, J-P. 1979: *From Munich to the Liberation 1938–1944*. Cambridge University Press.

Courtois, S. 1980: *Le Parti Communiste Français dans la guerre*. Ramsay.

Foot, M.R.D. 1966: *S.O.E. in France 1940–44*. H.M.S.O.

Foot, M.R.D. 1976: *Resistance*. Eyre Methuen.

De Gaulle, C. 1954 –:*Mémoires de Guerre*. 3 vols. Plon.

Gordon, B.M. 1980: *Collaborationism in France during the Second World War*. Cornell University Press.

Halls, W.D. 1981: *The Youth of Vichy France*. Clarendon Press.

Hawes, S. and White, R. (eds) 1975: *Resistance in Europe*. Allen Lane.

Hoffmann, S. 1974: *Decline or Renewal? France since the 1930s*. Viking.

Horne, A. 1964: *To Lose a Battle: France 1940*. Macmillan.

Kedward, H.R. 1978: *Resistance in Vichy France*. Oxford University Press.

Kedward, H. R. and Austin, R. (eds) 1985: *Vichy France and the Resistance*: Culture and Ideology. Croom Helm.

Knight, F. 1975: *The French Resistance 1940–44*. Lawrence & Wishart.

Marrus, M.R. and Paxton, R. 1981: *Vichy France and the Jews*. Basic Books.

Michel, H. 1970: *La Guerre de l'Ombre: la Résistance en Europe*. Grasset.

Michel, H. 1966: *Vichy: année 40*. Laffont.

Noguères, H. 1967 –: *Histoire de la Résistance en France de 1940 à 1945*, 5 vols. Laffont.

Ophuls, M. 1975: *The Sorrow and the Pity: a film script*. Berkeley Publishing Corporation.

Ory, P. 1976: *Les Collaborateurs 1940–45*. Éditions du Seuil.

Paxton, R. 1972: *Vichy France: Old Guard and New Order 1940–44*. Knopf.

Stafford, D. 1980: *Britain and European Resistance: a survey of the Special Operations Executive*. Macmillan.

Sweets, J.F. 1976: *The Politics of Resistance in France 1940–44*. Northern Illinois University Press.

Sweets, J. F. 1986: *Choices in Vichy France: the French under Nazi Occupation*. Oxford University Press.

Thomas, R.T. 1979: *Britain and Vichy: the dilemma of Anglo-French Relations 1940–42*. Macmillan.

Tillon, C. 1962: *Les F.T.P.* Julliard.

Warner, G. 1968: *Pierre Laval and the Eclipse of France*. Eyre and Spottiswoode.

Willard, G. 1972: *De la Guerre à la Libération*. Éditions Sociales.

References

Amouroux, H. 1977: *La Grande Histoire des Français sous l'Occupation.* Vol. 2, *Quarante millions de Pétainistes.* Laffont.

Austin, Roger 1983: The Chantiers de la Jeunesse in Languedoc, 1940–44. *French Historical Studies,* 8 no. 1.

Barthes, Roland 1957: *Mythologies.* Éditions du Seuil.

Brasillach, R. 1955: *Journal d'un homme Occupé.* Les Sept Couleurs.

Laborie, Pierre 1980: *Résistants, Vichyssois et autres.* CNRS.

Lytton, Neville 1942: *Life in Unoccupied France.* Macmillan.

Marrus, M.R. and Paxton, R. 1981: *Vichy France and the Jews.* Basic Books.

Maurras, Charles 1941: *La Seule France.* Lardanchet.

Simon, Paul 1942: *One Enemy Only – The Invader.* Hodder and Stoughton.

Vercors (Jean Bruller) 1942: *Le Silence de la mer.* Éditions de Minuit.

Index

85